Petrushka

Proceedings of a conference
on Severe Epidemic Phytonotic Syndrome (SEPS)

Held at Cape Cod, Massachusetts

Geneva 2017

ISBN 978-2-9700376-3-7

The parsley sample belongs to the Vavilov Institute of Plant Industry, St Petersburg, Russian Federation.
Title page of the Petrograd monograph on Fusarium courtesy of the Bibliothèque des Conservatoire et Jardin botaniques de la Ville de Genève, Switzerland.
Shuntaro Tanikawa, 'Tree', translated by William I. Elliott and Kazuo Kawamura, from *Selected Poems* (Manchester, Carcanet, 1998).
Vicki Feaver, 'Bramble Arm' by permission of the author.
Oliverio Girondo, 'Arborescencia' translated by PMcC.
Meng Chiao, 'Song of the Old Man of the Hills', translated by A.C. Graham, from *Poems of the Late T'ang* (Harmondsworth, Penguin Books, 1965).
Vladislav Khodasevich, 'Putem zerna' translated by PMcC.
Giuseppe Arcimboldo, *Vertumnus*, hangs in Skokloster Castle, Sweden.
Other photographs by Peter McCarey.
Design and typesetting by Gerry Cambridge
Set in Monotype Plantin

Published by Molecular Press, Geneva

NB: the meeting took place; the epidemic did not.

Cover Note

The Petrushka group was established to consider what might be done to combat SEPS (Severe Epidemic Phytonotic Syndrome) if technology fails or exacerbates the condition. Whilst its origin is uncertain, SEPS seems to thrive on electromagnetic radiation of every kind. The meeting was therefore convened by post, participants made their way to Cape Cod by land and water, and had to rely on their own knowledge, since on-line resources were not accessible. Some who were invited did not arrive, so there are gaps in expertise that we could not supply. We did place one long call to an epidemiologist engaged in the technological fight against SEPS, because thoughts emerging from a total information blackout would surely have been inept. As it is, recommendations are tentative, since we do not know how far the plague has spread, or which societies and communities have been disabled. The competing priorities of medicine, public health, ecosystems and biology were discussed, but the group did not ultimately arbitrate among them. This is partly because the situation is in flux. It is possible also that, rather like old colonial powers, humans are incapable of envisaging a course of action in which they do not have the leading role.

Three typed copies of these proceedings are being sent to the Assembly by three different roads.

We thank our hosts, Laura Frader and Jim Cronin.

The group wishes to thank the Rockefeller Foundation Bellagio Centre, without which the meeting could not have been convened.

Contents

Participants

Caterina Borelli, independent director/producer for documentaries and television, Rome/NewYork City
Mariarosaria Cardines, linguist, Geneva
James Cronin, Professor of History, Boston College
Laura Frader, Professor of History, Northeastern University, works on labor, gender inequality and social policy in France
Eric Hamlin, software engineer, Los Angeles
Elysa Hammond, Director of Environmental Stewardship, Clif Bar
Peter McCarey, Convenor and Chair, Geneva
Douglas Maclean, Professor of Philosophy, University of North Carolina, works on ethics, political philosophy, and public policy
Charles M. Peters, tropical ecologist, forester, Kate E. Tod Curator of Botany at the New York Botanical Garden
Stephen Rapp, former national and international prosecutor; 2009–2015 US ambassador-at-large for global criminal justice
Dr. Jesus Ramirez-Valles, Professor and Head of Community Health Sciences, University of Illinois at Chicago
Susan Vo, report writer, Calgary

Preparatory meeting

Christopher Harvie, Professor of History, Tübingen University
Dr Patrik Buchmüller, Tübingen University
John Clifford, Austrian Honorary Consul in Edinburgh
Dr Patricia Conlan, Irish Law Association, Dublin
Frank Conlan, Dublin
Representative Jacob Lund, Member of the Folketing, Denmark

Advisers

Arkady Borisovich Aref'ev, Bol'shaja Rechka, Siberia
John Broome, Emeritus White's Professor of Moral Philosophy at the University of Oxford
Anastasia Gavrilina, Herzen Institute, St Petersburg
Olesya Val'ger, Novosibirsk

(ii) *Revision of the Draft Agenda*

On 1 July the 26th Freudenstadt Symposium on European Regionalism hosted a fringe meeting to prepare the agenda for the Cape Cod conference. With further refinements proposed in the Hebrides later that month, it was adopted after slight amendment by the conference (see Meeting Report).

The Freudenstadt meeting was to have been addressed by a prominent SEPS campaigner, who succumbed to the syndrome en route. Her draft speaking notes are reproduced below, *in memoriam:*

Dear Colleagues,

Since the initial case appeared – or rather since what is generally taken as the initial case appeared – we have been overwhelmed. Nothing seems to stop it; you name it and it's been tried: defoliant, radical surgery, organic farming, Jungian psychotherapy and ikebana.

What caused it? Where did it come from? Again, we don't know. The usual suspects keep coming up: big pharma, big government, something emerging from the Himalayan forest with climate change, tourism, terrorism, refugees, the future. Yes, the future – more on that one later.

What are the precedents? Well, not so long ago, the so-called 'tree man'; much further back – lichen which is, after all, a form of symbiosis. Though we might even imagine it began as a similarly violent attack of one kingdom on another before the two sides came to a modus vivendi. Much further back still, there is mitochondrial DNA. Yes, the motor of our own cells might have been a foreign body only gradually assimilated and put to use. Then of course there are the echoes in human cultures – many many stories of people suddenly turning into various types of vegetation. Although strangely none in the part of the world where this phenomenon actually seems to have surfaced. Sorry, I'm getting ahead of myself here.

The main thrust in the fight against SEPS is being led by the Assembly and a congeries of public-private partnerships. The disabling effects of the disease seem to be compounded by electromagnetic radiation, on which almost all information depends. The fight-back entails redoubling and intensifying the use of IT, putting as many people as possible under total 24/7 observation, offering good treatment in exchange for central governance of all their personal and biological data, now and in the future. We have to hope they succeed.

If they do not succeed then the importance of this, the off-line group, takes on extraordinary significance. We are or will be confronted with two questions: (1) What can be done for the general population and for the refugees? (2) What do we want to save?

What I mean is this. In 1941 the USSR issued to partisans a booklet on how to survive in nature while fighting the enemy: what plants, berries and roots to eat and how to prepare them. This was with a view to winning a war in which supplies were fraught. In the USA these days there are the survivalists, people who have retreated into remote areas with their munitions, subsistence farming and precious metals.

My view is that if we are reduced to this, then we have already lost the fight. Some of you will disagree and you shall have a chance to speak. Some of you will go farther and say that humanity doesn't have to survive; something will live on after we have gone. Well, it seems that krill has roughly the same biomass as humanity. They would probably survive. But I can't help feeling that a species whose purpose in life seems to be that of bringing minerals into an edible shape for whales can't be seen as a consolation for the disappearance of civilization.

So I repeat, we have two topics for discussion, at least one of which must result in specific recommendations for action: how can we protect the population, fixed and mobile, with 20th-century techniques? And what precisely do we aim to protect in terms of science and culture?

Vladimir Kondratiev presented at a clinic in Phuket during a family holiday in the second week of January this year, having taken a six-hour charter flight from Abakan in central Siberia. He was evacuated immediately to Bangkok General Hospital, where he underwent X-ray and CAT examination. By this time he was in severe pain, which examination seemed to exacerbate. A local specimen of bamboo (*Bambusa blumeana* — *(phai si suk)* — *Blume's Giant Thorny Bamboo*) had taken root in his right side, between two ribs. Unfortunately for the subject, the plant that attacked him is perhaps the fastest-growing organism on earth, and this specimen grew at the rate of almost 4cm per hour. Before a course of treatment could be decided the bamboo had implanted itself in his lungs, which made complex, radical surgery an urgent necessity. The patient was, as it happened, in one of the best surgical centres in the region, and he did pull through, much reduced physically.

Within 24 hours of his emergence from general anaesthetic two further, deadly consequences were observed, each engendering further complications: several new seedlings broke through the skin at various parts of the patient's body. Whereas they were successfully removed, it became apparent that the non-invasive examinations caused pain and discomfort. There was also the suspicion, never thereafter dispelled, that those examinations boosted the growth of the vegetation. The second consequence was contraction by both surgeons, by the scrub nurses and by two ward nurses, of similar complaints; similar because they entailed phytonotic attacks, though by different species of plant.

In all cases it proved possible to uproot each plant as it was detected, and while it was technically possible to keep each new patient under observation with a view to further surgical treatment, in no case was full remission achieved in that first phase, and the hospital quickly found its medical and logistic resources exhausted. This situation was soon replicated at treatment centres throughout Bangkok. Bangkok is, of course, one of the busiest airport hubs in south-east Asia, with direct flights to every major airport on Earth.

Information suffered is disease. An epidemic is the onset of information whose intensity, complexity or strangeness overwhelms established information management structures such as people and civilizations.

What emanated from Bangkok General was an electromagnetic flash that could not prepare other centres for the morbid shockwave to follow. Email and video documented surgical procedures that seemed to transmit the pathogen in the attempt to stop its rampant effects.

Email and video did not transmit the syndrome itself. However, once it took root it photosynthesized, drawing on ambient electromagnetic radiation, which did include the energy of smart phones and of scanning and diagnostic equipment.

For those reasons, and rapidly, emergency rooms emptied of all but those who suffered too much to stay put, and who could still move. Transmission was fast but random; a large but undefined proportion of any given population was immune. Researchers knew neither the transmission path, nor what conferred immunity, nor indeed what the lucky ones were immune to.

Fusarium? – No. Carrion flowers? In a sense each case of SEPS was a carrion plant, but only in the terminal phase, which was not always reached, because some hosts came to a symbiotic or commensal arrangement with their guests.

In view of the immense difference in outcome produced by different plants, people began to hold the equivalent of 'measles parties', in which parents had tried to ensure their children caught the disease early, to avoid complications later. People filled their dwellings with slow-growing, shallow-rooted plants. They spoke to them as they would to delinquent grandchildren.

Some tried to weaponize the epidemic; a number of detention centres turned to forests; bamboo groves appeared at strategic points.

Time of death was difficult to establish since technically death supervened not on expiry of the human host but on dessication of the autotroph. This, and environmental considerations, ruled out cremation. Small plantations appeared, haphazard at first, then downwind of every human settlement. After some hesitation dictated by various cultural scruples, harvesting of fruit and grains became the norm.

The hunt for a causative agent continued. What could be smaller and simpler than a virus? A line of binary. There was nothing in nature that changed the iron atom in haemoglobin to the magnesium atom in chlorophyll, but 'replace iron with magnesium' was on the face of it a simple enough instruction for a machine.

Prior to the epidemic much of the adolescent population had been reduced to a vegetative state by virtual reality. Was this simply one step further? Could it be that the epidemic drew information as well as energy from the cloud?

An epidemiologist was asked for advice; he responded with the following set of questions, to which provisional answers have been given. It is proposed that the epidemiologist guide discussion of the relevant item.

STRATEGY

What do we KNOW is happening, who, how, when and where?
We know that since January SEPS has spread from south-east Asia to every continent, affecting up to 30% of any population group it touches. Since the latency period of infection varies from days to several months or perhaps more, the 30% proportion must be regarded as a provisional ceiling. Humans and domestic animals affected by SEPS become host to any wild species of plant or fungus. In both animal and vegetable kingdoms, the line between 'domestic' and 'wild' is conceptually ill-defined. In practice, it is determined by aptitude to host or cause SEPS.

We know that a common sign of SEPS is shame and a desire to conceal its effects; people also tend to go off line rapidly to avoid electromagnetic radiation.

What do we THINK is happening, who, how, when and where?
For the above reasons, much is in the realm of speculation. We think that natural immunity is associated with one particular enterotype of the gut microbiome in humans. It would seem to be an ecosystem hostile to SEPS. This is the most promising line of research for treatment. The case-fatality rate of SEPS is high but until systematic surveys can be conducted in pilot populations we will not have a percentage. A huge variety of improvised cures is being attempted, largely without documentation, and some are likely to work. Staying in total darkness for several days should kill plant seedlings, though it will expose people to fungal attack. Exposing seedlings to hostile environ-

ments should work in many cases, though the process can be vexatious. Tropical plants, for example, cannot withstand refrigeration, but nor can their human hosts. Simple weed killer (such as sodium chlorate) will kill off many species of plant, but necrotic tissue remains that requires rapid, expert surgery, which brings its own worries. Genetically modified pesticide has wider implications, discussed under 'elimination'.

How can we CONFIRM what we think is happening is correct?
Faith-based broadcasting from arid deserts and from farmland where only genetically modified corn is grown confirm that the absence or weakness of wild plants does offer a considerable degree of protection. It is however unlikely that such broadcasts would draw attention to an outbreak in those environments. Sandy coastal areas such as Cape Cod are auspicious. The fact that the index case was in south-central Siberia, which is as far from the sea as it is possible to get on this planet, may suggest that sodium chloride rather than sodium chlorate would confer some protection.
In short, we can confirm little at this juncture.

What do we think WILL happen if we do nothing?
Assume 30% prevalence with 50% case fatality, and survivors reluctant to engage with society.

What are the consequences?
A power-grab by established and startup religions and makers of genetically modified organisms. General recourse to mafia-style management techniques.

What public health interventions are possible/feasible?
For the moment, the only proven cure is radical surgery, which is not a public health intervention. Also, surgeons are insisting on remote, robotic operations, which few can afford. Research must therefore focus on (1) the microbiome and (2) the influence of saline environments.

Are we aiming for control, elimination or eradication? CAN it be controlled/eradicated?
Eradication could be envisaged only through drastic reduction of plant diversity. This is being pursued in some areas but must be opposed. Elimination is not yet on the horizon. Containment is an aspirational goal.

What should we tell people and how and when (the public, healthcare workers, etc)?
Since surgery is the only proven means of cure and since it has become too expensive for all but a very few, the attendant dangers and uncertainties must be stressed in public health messaging.
Insist on the long-term need for species diversity.
Work on returning survivors to active life in the community.

How do we know if we are managing to contain it?
Societal collapse is avoided.

At what stage, and based on what criteria, do we introduce more draconian measures to control it?
Unauthorized draconian measures have already been introduced, unsystematically, at every level of society.

At what stage, and based on what criteria, do we stop trying to control it, eliminate it or eradicate it?
No answer.

At what stage, and based on what criteria, do we look to saving the species with extreme actions (space missions, undersea civilisations, etc)?
Such measures should be planned and costed as of now. Colonization of the seabed and neighbouring planets, and re-population of sinking Pacific islands. If even these fail, we might contemplate progressive taxation to fund public health.

TACTICS

What can protect people from being exposed (at individual and community level)?
Living in arid zones, at high altitude or on the sea.
Possibly built-up areas and certain monoculture farms.

How can we protect individuals/communities already exposed?
Check, case by case, what conditions acceptable to the host are inimical to the plant.

How do we/can we help individuals who are sick with the disease?
Recruit those who are naturally immune as carers.

Do we need any special management of dead bodies?
Yes. No cremation; if possible, special beds away from dwellings, but without insisting on removal of bodies/plants from homes where they are being tended.

This would not be the first epidemic to threaten or cause the collapse of entire populations: Spanish influenza globally, smallpox in the Americas, plague in Europe. It is certain that others, though equally momentous, have gone unrecorded. SEPS or something like it might have been with us before.

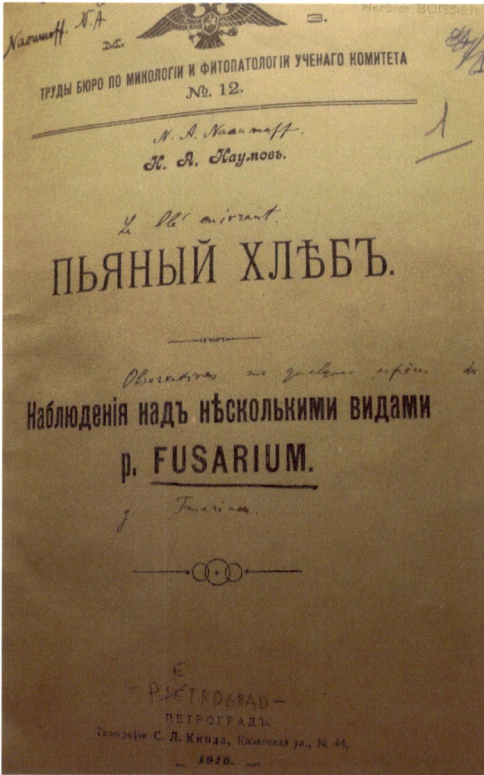

The fungus Fusarium is known to infest both plants and animals, and a paper published in Petrograd in 1916 describes it as a saprophyte with strong parasitic traits – which certainly fits the behaviour of SEPS.

There is also *Epidermodysplasia verruciformis*, 'tree-man disease', but this is a rare form of human papillomavirus that is not of the vegetable kingdom. There are many clinical states classed as vegetative, though here we are in the realm of metaphor: such people have not been colonized by the vegetable kingdom, but rather present behaviour and passivity reminiscent of plants.

Where does metaphor end and fact begin?

Each human carries an astonishing quantity and variety of what until recently was called intestinal flora, and the working hypothesis is that that is what in some prevents and in others causes development of SEPS.

Metaphor aside, haemoglobin and chlorophyll are not dissimilar: a ring of carbon, hydrogen and nitrogen with a metal in the middle – iron for haemoglobin, magnesium for chlorophyll. Until now, though, each has kept to its own domain.

We must ask ourselves whether we are witnessing an epochal change, such as happened when mitochondrial DNA was coopted into our ancestor cells two billion years ago and put to use. If so, should we allow it? Can we prevent it? What exactly do we wish to defend – the human organism, the biotope, both or not necessarily either?

The gods, in legend, change shape at will. Human metamorphosis is catastrophic and irreversible. That difference is a function of mortality.

Accounts of people turning into plants are found in clusters: legends are linked to specific sites in the Mediterranean world; unexplained depictions of a 'Green Man', often ornamenting Christian churches, are found from the Atlantic to Central Russia; and there are vast regions where no such thing is apparent – Siberia and the far north.

Relevant information on the Americas, Africa and East Asia would be welcome.

Going on what we have for the moment, the Siberian silence is eloquent. While it is as difficult in the arts as in the sciences to secure a negative proof, we would suggest that shamanistic metamorphoses concern birds and animals, not plants. Siberian legends, and artifacts in Russian museums, bear this out. (And Peter the Great's Kunstkamera, which collected natural anomalies throughout the Russian Empire, contains no evidence of phytonosis.)

The Green Man motif tells us nothing. Roslyn Chapel in Scotland contains over a hundred carvings of heads spouting vegetation, and the portal of the church of St Dmitri, in Vladimir, depicts dozens of smiling heads with branches growing from their crown, but in contrast to Christian imagery on the same walls, no stable tradition attaches a meaning to them. A 19th-century study of Roslyn, in the library of nearby Hawthornden Castle, doesn't mention them. It is likely that the motif is simply part of the Romanesque decorative vernacular, an 'animal, vegetable, mineral' trope of no great relevance to our subject.

With Ovid's *Metamorphoses* we are on much more fertile ground, for several reasons: the poem lists dozens of detailed cases of outlandish transformations; at the same time (in book VII) it offers an account of an epidemic and the attendant societal collapse that could find its place in a medical journal; finally, some of the metamorphoses it describes are found in other languages, thousands of years later and thousands of miles away.

There are about twenty cases of vegetative transformation in the poem. If we set aside the etiological tales (which explain why the mulberry is red, why frankincense is pungent and why reeds whisper), all but one are cases of somatization: extreme distress triggers a physical crisis so severe that the individual is reduced to an emblem of his or her condition. For the poet, the essential metamorphosis is in that transcendence. For us it is in the physical transformation.

Metamorphosis into flowers and small plants seems quick and painless: the narcissus, violet, crocus and hyacinth *just happen*. For the laurel, lotus and myrrh tree, the cypress and the oak, it's another matter: it always starts with the feet and the trunk; the lips are always last to be overcome.

In book I, a woman fleeing a would-be rapist calls on the gods to rescue her; she turns into a laurel tree. There is a relentless emphasis on speed in this incident: both the woman and her attacker are moving unnaturally fast. If we slow it all down we see a woman under threat of sexual violence who transforms her body, perhaps anorexically, into something that would repel attackers.

Almost all the remaining metamorphoses can be similarly reduced to somatization of fear, grief, rage or love. Almost all. In book IX, a woman plucks a lotus flower, which starts to bleed. Unwittingly she has damaged a nymph who had been metamorphosed into a flower. The woman is warped and distended into a tree. So this is not a somatic mutation: it is an infection, and it recurs elsewhere, through Dante's Italy to the USA: the black branch dripping blood, the strange fruit.

These things are real or they are true, never both at once.

Jesus heals a blind man and asks him what he sees.
'I see men, because I see what looks like walking trees.' (Mark, 8:24).
(Curious: Jesus earns his crust as a carpenter and returns as a gardener; living wood for dead.)

The Scottish poet Hugh MacDiarmid writes:

> 'Aye this is Calvary: to bear
> Your Cross wi'in you frae the seed
> And feel it grow by slow degrees
> Until it rends your flesh apairt...

—A Drunk Man Looks at the Thistle

Such transformations are not always regarded with horror. It is clear enough that the stories themselves can fortify or even exhilarate, and that they mutate. The change is welcomed or simply accepted:

Baucis and Philemon, *Metamorphosis* book VIII: Old couple providing a meal for divine beings travelling incognito (echoes of Abraham and Sarah) who save them from the flood (echoes of Gilgamesh) and are in the end changed into two entwining trees (reprised in the death of Tristan and Isolde, in the ballad of Barbara Allen, and in stories from here to Hawaii – (the story of Lehua and Ohi'a)). A Chinese version,'A Peacock Flew', dates from the 3rd to 5th century AD; see Arthur Waley, *Chinese Poems* (London, 1946, p.89).

In contemporary literature there is another category of poem which makes no reference to the Ovidian or related tradition and which, in view of SEPS, might be regarded as prodromal rather than literary in meaning. Such texts are to be found at random throughout the world. Four examples should suffice to illustrate the point (see below). What, if anything, is to be made of this, is for the meeting to discuss.

Arborescence

I thought it was a rebellious hair,
twisted,
but when I looked at my chest
I saw it was green.

Nights and days passed.
A little leaf appeared
then another... and another...
and yet another.

A four-leafed clover?
What fun!
Such joy!

But as the months died,
hard bark covered its trunk,
while a few branches grew.

Now it's a solitary,
branchy,
perfect,
tiny little tree.

—Oliverio Girondo (Argentina)

A sheep tick engorged in my forearm,
Its wings like an artichoke leaves sticking up?
but here's the trick: it was a cyclamen.
Now root it up gently; there's
Barely a graze,
There's hardly a tic of discomfort,
And carry it, rinky tink tink, to the house.
Is that borage or cress on my bicep?

—Peter McCarey (Scotland/Switzerland)

Tree

Pretty soon I'll be a tree.
The tip of my middle finger tingles
and sprouts green leaves.
And then I find that
other leaves grow out of my ring finger, index finger,
and my arms fork into limber branches .
Inside my shirt my body
becomes a
rugged trunk.
My toes dissolve into mud
and tepid water creeps up to my lower belly.
I quit going to school.
I quit playing baseball, quit fishing.
I just stand still, even at night.
Rain refreshes me.
No one notices me at all.

They just hurry by.
Until the day I fade I go nowhere.
I keep on rustling, swaying in the wind.

—Shuntaro Tanikawa (Japan)

Bramble Arm

In a dream, my right arm –
the arm that wields

my writing hand –
is encircled by brambles,

coiled from elbow to wrist
like barbed wire.

It could be a punishment
for writing in the voice

I was taught as a child
to soften or silence.

or maybe it's a sign
of its power – my weak

woman's arm transformed
into a fearsome weapon.

Later in the dream, the arm
is swathed in bandages,

as if to hide or smother
the barbs. But the gauze

is stained with blood
and blackberry juice.

Under the wrapping
the bramble still lives:

roots twined round
sinew and bone;

spiked shoots
piercing the flesh.

—Vicki Feaver (England)

Finally, two more, from farther back:

Song of the Old Man of the Hills

I never go to the plains beneath the hills,
Only on the hillside plant my fields.
The hatchet at my waist chops down the pines in the copse,
The gourd in my hand draws water from the homestead spring.
What do I care for the force of written words
Let no one heed the shifts of sun and moon.
When the twisted tree at last shall be my body
Then I shall begin to live out my natural span.

—Meng Chiao, 751–814

The Way of the Grain

The sower walks across the furrowed field
Where father and grandfather both have toiled.

The grain of wheat is golden in his hand
But it must fall into the black black ground,

And it shall, where the blind worm makes its road,
At the allotted hour, die and grow.

And my soul too will go the way of the grain:
Down in the dark to die, and live again.

And you, my country, and you, her folk,
Will die and live again. The year is dark

And the only wisdom, our only sign:
The living all must go the way of the grain.

—Vladislav Khodasevich

Summary

The remit of this group specifically excludes attribution of the cause of this epidemic to commercial or political agency, and to positing a causal connection with mass tourism, mass migration or climate change per se. Such subjects are for the Assembly to manage.

Nevertheless there is one epiphenomenon peculiar to SEPS that does concern causality, if only as an expression of societal angst, and this is the scattering of individuals who claim that SEPS has been engineered by future generations of humans who have taken this drastic step in order to avert the catastrophe that – they say – will obliterate much of the biosphere unless current human activity is curtailed. A few of them claim to have travelled back in time to oversee the implantation of SEPS. In this they are reminiscent of members of apocalyptic sects of the early modern period who claimed to be the reincarnation of some founding saint of their movement.

An interview with one of them is attached to this document. Members are asked to consider whether any response seems appropriate, bearing in mind that leaders of apocalyptic movements have been known to cause or exacerbate major upheavals, whether or not that was their stated or conscious purpose.

Annex

– Mr...
– Inspector.
– Inspector, yes. Thank you for agreeing to this interview. Would you tell me where you have come from, please, and for what purpose.

– I come from the same place, really, just 4° ahead.

– 4°?

– We no longer measure things in revolutions around the sun, but in gross ambient temperature above absolute zero. I have come to this juncture for two reasons, one trivial, the other not. I wanted to eat something other than jellyfish, and you still have a lot of vertebrate species left here, in and out of the water. So I volunteered for the rather more consequent mission of overseeing a scheme to redress the ecological balance a few generations hence. This is being done through the introduction to this juncture of, well, of what you refer to as SEPS.

– Rather a drastic measure.

– Long reflected. No alternative found.

– But isn't there a logical paradox that precludes future action on earlier time?

– No.

– What about the grandfather paradox.

– Which is?

– That if you, say, travelled fifty years back in time and married your grandmother, you would then be your own grandfather!

– Are you saying that the incest taboo prevails over the laws of physics? The audience will love that!

– The audience?

– Well this is *all* being monitored. Indeed, in an important respect I'm not here at all – just a projection of many coordinated aspects of oneself. We haven't yet overcome the problem of what you call jet lag. Between time zones it's unpleasant; across time it can take the form of a suicidal hangover.

– If this succeeds you may find no one to go back to.

– And if it fails the future looks bad anyway. Thanks for your concern, but you've asked me to speak about the current situation, so let's not digress.

– Alright. You claim to have caused one of the deadliest epidemics in human history. How can you ever justify that?

– Your own philosophers do the same: the worth of lives in distant future generations is discounted in calculations of value. We have simply reciprocated.

– I'm sorry, I'm not a philosopher and I don't understand that. You claim to have introduced an element to our ecology that is killing countless innocent people.

– So if you believed what I said you would have me arraigned for mass murder or genocide. But I speak to you in full confidence that you don't believe me at all. So if you'll excuse me ... (interview ends).

Before Bangkok General Hospital shut down it was quarantined, and before it was quarantined it had transmitted much information about the onset and treatment of SEPS to major hospitals around the world. Experts knew what to look for in patients, but had no clue as to what triggered the outbreak. Vladimir Kondratiev's contacts were traced back to the transit lounge at BKK, where CCTV showed he had (literally) bumped into an American forester, contracted by the Government of Myanmar to advise on and supervise sustainable forestry projects in the north-east of the country – Himalayan piedmont that is some of the least accessible terrain on Earth, for several reasons: poor roads, violence over control of heroin, jade and cross-border smuggling, population displacement, and a generous variety of neurotoxic and haematoxic reptiles.

The UN agency tasked with responding to the outbreak was, as luck would have it, in the process of re-electing its director, whose first action was to relocate the relevant meeting to another country, to be sure that the ministers who had promised to vote for him would be able to do so. The agency's communications department focused on explaining this decision to the standing committee on reform and to the general public.

It therefore took the international community longer than normal to assemble a team that could go to the region and look for cases, which they duly found, spreading out from the village in which the American forester, and his replacement, had worked and was working.

The task of recording and describing the cases was unimaginably fraught: the transmission path at that stage seemed random, with high odds of contracting the syndrome. Team members did not know how to protect themselves. They were rotated out of the danger zone and into quarantine and observation after two-week spells. In the course of their investigations they encountered almost as many new plant species as they did new cases of SEPS. It was therefore impossible to know whether a given plant found rooted in a patient was in its normal state or not. The importance of this was the working assumption that behind the first case of SEPS in humans there lay a fateful mutation in some species of plant.

They were, we now believe, barking up the wrong tree, in the wrong country.

Vladimir had indeed bumped into the American forester who had just left that part of the forest in the Himalayan foothills. A few minutes later, that forester had lunched with the colleague who was heading north to take over from him in the forestry project. It had been running for three of its projected five years, and the two of them spelled each other as local project manager. The replacement left BKK after lunch on a Yangon flight, carrying the causative agent. The cases found in the jungle by the investigation team when they got there two weeks later, were fanning out in front of them. The source of the outbreak was not in the forest but in Vladimir.

How do we know this? And why is it not common knowledge? First question first.

In the deadly struggle being waged at Bangkok General Hospital, recovery of data from Vladimir's smart phone was not a priority. When it did occur to someone to use that data to confirm the hypothesis, there was the problem of Vladimir's mental state. This was or had been an intelligent 15-year-old boy, looking forward to his first family holiday abroad and his first visit to a really foreign, really hot country. Within days he was in extreme pain and confusion, and thereafter was in constant fear of death, without the immediate comfort of his family. By the time he was in a stable condition the hospital around him was not. He had probably forgotten his password and was not in a state to permit others to try to gain access to his personal files. He had been using proprietary software from one country that was licensed for use in another, with reservations on access, privacy etc.. It took a few months to gain access to his social media profile, which afforded the kind of trivia one would expect of a teenage boy. Investigations focused on the days before his trip and found nothing. He had been wandering round his district of Abakan, in south central Siberia, doing last-minute shopping for sun cream and running errands for his mother. This had taken him to the central market, a large outdoor area near the bus station, with narrow, icy pathways between rows of temporary stalls selling clothing, hardware, fruit and vegetables.

There had recently been a major change in the supply of fresh produce, Kyrgyz farms stepping in to replace the perishables now covered by Western sanctions. No lead there: Kyrgyzstan had not been among the first or second wave of countries reporting cases.

On perhaps the fifth viewing of some mock video documentary that Vladimir had done with his friend at the market, he was pointing at an old lady selling herbs. 'Where did she get fresh parsley?' he was saying. 'She's from around here, my grandmother knows her'. He pointed to or handled a bunch and said 'where's this from?' She chased him away. It was a good question.

Instructions were sent for a local inspector to investigate. By now it was early spring; this market, like most public places then, had few sellers and few buyers. But since some people had to choose between possible infection and certain hunger, the few kept coming. These included the old lady, who was selling a range of dried herbs, including dried parsley. She claimed no recollection of Vladimir – even though he had become the town's most famous son – and said that the only parsley she ever sold in winter was, of course, dried or preserved. The inspector report back and that was that. Not quite. Viewing the video again our researcher was not convinced; he asked for more information on the woman, beginning with her address.

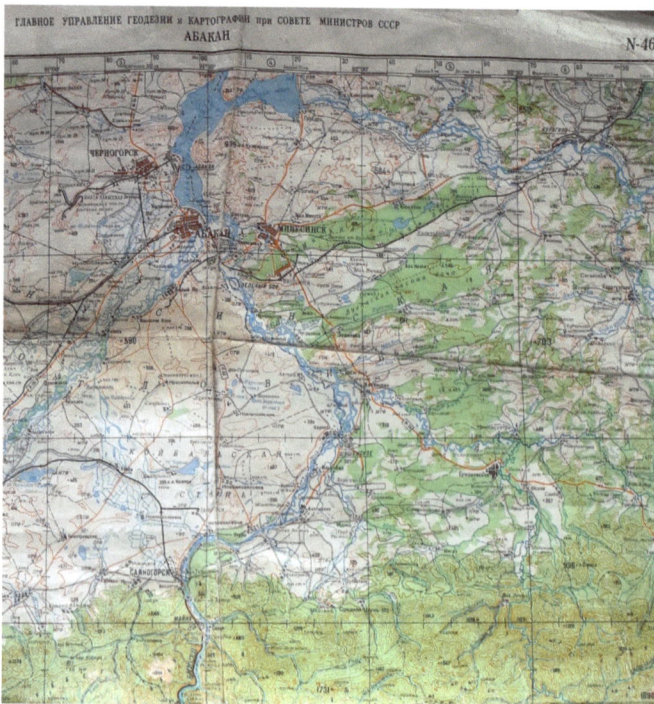

So I found out where she lived: east of Moscow, north of Bangkok, on a tributary of the mighty Yenisei that divides Russia in two. About as far away from the ocean as it is possible to get on planet Earth and – at a more banal level – not all that easy to reach from Abakan: it took between six hours and two days, depending on connections which, these days, aren't great.

I had three hours between the train and the noon bus to Ermakovskoye. So I had kasha and black tea in the scrupulously clean 1960s waiting room, which was staffed by a lady from the neighbouring Tuva Republic, who assured me that shamanism had nothing to do with this epidemic whether as cause or as cure. Three immense locomotives hummed past, pulling a line of wagons that was longer than our conversation. I passed through the market (still in operation) and on to the bus station. Another clean café, selling nothing fresh.

A lady had covered the front of her kiosk with perhaps 150 little dolls and toy cars retailing at a few roubles each. Her customers were all men and she was purveying some type of liquid refreshment that wasn't advertised. Apologies: these days the eye takes in more detail than it needs for fear of missing something precious or perilous.

At Ermakovskoye, several more hours in a bright waiting room, iron-framed windows above benches along two walls; a lady carefully mopping the tiled floor that was a decade behind in repairs. Toilet outside, across the ancient ice of the bus park, consisted of a corrugated iron screen around a wooden platform with rectangular holes above the pit. Too cold for flies. The bus arrived, couched high on its axles, deep treaded tyres. It took us through the village of Razezhe and over the first of two passes – a climb of just 300 metres, but easily made impossible by ice and snow. The second pass was blocked; no barricade, just a wall of snow that had been pushed up from the other side to a height of three metres. The bus returned to Razezhe.

Razezhe means 'the parting of the ways', or 'fanning out'; it was once the point at which hunters split up, each taking his own agreed direction into the taiga. Then Belaya Rechka had been built, further in, over those last two passes, as a holiday village for forestry workers (who also hunted).

When the logging had stopped after the economic collapse of the 1990s, some people had nowhere else to go. By now 70%

of the villagers were retired and living on shrinking pensions. It would seem that they had agreed to shut themselves in.

I went into the general store at Razezhe, bought a few items I didn't need, and told the owner I had been intending to visit some people in Belaya Rechka. He advised against it: 'once a gang of Chinese poachers moved in on BR; no one figured out where they stayed while they were there, but a lot of sticky polythene traps appeared that caught all the frogs and snakes. The local hunters weren't directly interested in them, but the sable and otter they hunted were. So they caught up with the poachers and explained to them (no Chinese interpretation was needed) that these things were carbines and that at times they went off by accident, and it would be dreadful if a poacher got shot by mistake.

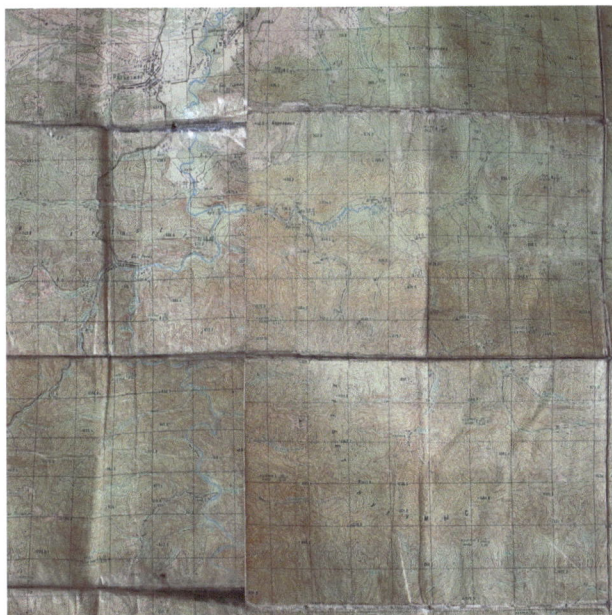

The poachers disappeared, but this left me with two further problems: I too might have an accident if I insisted, and the very purpose of my visit was somewhat undermined if the poacher story was not simply one more expression of Russian fear of demographic pressure. What if, rather than originating in BR, the phytonosis had been imported via Mongolia and Tuvinia from an unspecified part of China?

Without explaining too much I told the shopkeeper that I would like at least to talk to the hunters who were now guarding the village, if there were a post I might approach. He said there was a hunting lodge off to the west and south, over the higher pass from Razezhe, that I might try. His nephew might even be persuaded to accompany me. He himself was clearly curious as to what was going on. I say 'hunting lodge' but don't get grand ideas: this would have been a log cabin with space for four berths, an iron stove and kit, a couple of icons of the Virgin and a local saint. They had been in the process of building a bath house next to it. The nephew and I started out the following morning. The days were getting longer but the paths were still clogged, and not all the frozen rivers could be walked across; some springs that welled up never froze at all. It was mostly birch wood and what they call cedar, Siberian pine, never very dense, on ancient eroded hills. The taiga. The only colour was the occasional bright red shock of cranberries at head height, cold and refreshing, honed by the frost since autumn. And some blood in the snow. The nephew – Ivan – said we had to follow it. 'One of the hunters?'

'No, these are elk tracks.'

'Can't we let it go?'

'Hunters never leave an animal wounded; if you're not sure of killing an animal you don't shoot, and if you do you go after it. You wouldn't want to cross the path of a wounded beast.'

'We just did. How far are we from the lodge?'

Since it was only fifteen minutes we agreed to go there first and get help in pursuing the animal. Ivan wanted to know why they hadn't pursued it in the first place.

The lodge was in a dell that we approached from the north. Two things. There was no wind but both of us heard the resonant undertone that high wind can produce when it meets an obstacle. And the dell was flooded in living green and lilac. Two chainsaws lay near the half-built bath hut. Sawdust, woodchip, jerry cans and tin mugs lay around. There was no sign of human life, just this feeding frenzy of lilac, which so spooked us both that I admit we did not try to enter the bothy.

Ivan wouldn't go on. I wasn't for turning back after coming so far. He explained that, after the dip, my path led down to the river, which I had to cross then follow upstream for ten kilometres. 'You can't miss it', he said, a statement I've often proved wrong. But not this time. Mid afternoon I got there and to my great good fortune the first people I happened on hadn't been keen on the idea of isolating the village, and were as welcoming as people can be in that part of the world. So once again, the combination of normalcy and terror that typifies this pandemic, or this stage of it at least. Goats in the kitchen, Mongolian ponies foraging in the street (the only street), not bothered by the number of hunting dogs on the loose or barking behind fences.

Sitting in the bath house with my host, he explained that though not actually a priest he was entrusted with the essential rituals in the absence of a real one. Also for guidance on pagan lore such as living and dead water. The temperature in the bath house was 110°C; the capillaries in my nose and lips felt set to explode, so I missed a lot of detail that it didn't seem right to return to, especially since my real interest was the old lady and her source of *petrushka*, parsley.

The minister, Arseny, said it would not be possible to visit her and her brother, but that he, as her only visitor, could tell me what I needed to know, which was this.

The woman's name was Evdokia, her brother was (another) Ivan. He had always been a drinker but when he lost his job in the forestry department he took it to new levels. Eventually he never emerged from their bath house; just lay there all day every day demanding drink and food, which his sister brought him, in ever diminishing quantities, because there was only so much she could get. One day she noticed he was scratching his forearm.

The minister explained that hygiene in the village is good. Granted, pit toilets in the gardens were alive with flies in the warm weather, but every cottage had its own *banya* (bath house), and if your body is routinely subjected to temperatures that range from -40° to +100°, bugs don't stand much of a chance. But Ivan's *banya*, where he lived, was constantly tepid, like a greenhouse. That was probably why he had started growing parsley. 'On his arms?' On his arms. Evdokia was getting desperate for funds, her dried herbs weren't competing well at market with fresh produce from Kyrgyzstan, so she had started harvesting the parsley and selling it in Abakan.

Evdokia no longer allowed even the minister in to visit, but she assured him her brother was as usual complaining and demanding drink and food, though only meat these days.

I was obliged to leave it at that. I was in the village under Arseny's protection and had to promise not to attempt a visit. I could have asked for a sample, but I thought it better to bring this information back to you rather than bring or attempt to bring the primary germ of this pandemic. We know where to look, if ever a cure is found.

Herbal cells may settle down and parasitize on the organism of a human or an animal
Geneticists say that mutations seriously change the set of chromosomes, and people with mutations can thus hardly be called humans. In Yerevan in the former Soviet republic of Armenia, 18-year-old girl Narine Aivasyan shocked doctors with her unusual disease. The girl complained about an abscess on her wrist that had been hurting her for a long period already. When doctors opened the bandage on Narine's hand they saw two very thin thorns sticking out of the hand.

The girl failed to enter a higher education institution after she left school, and had to help her mother about the house and assisted her in a store where the woman worked. The girl was fond of pot plants and devoted much time to looking after her plants. Once, Narine pricked herself on a cactus while watering plants. Some thorns got stuck in her wrist. The parents immediately disinfected the wound but it still festered and even expanded. Narine was reluctant to visit a doctor. She had to go to a hospital in a month when a point of a thorn emerged on the skin right on the place of the red wound. Doctors easily removed the strange object, but more thorns turned up on the same spot soon.

Head of the immunology and virology laboratory at the Armenia research center Tigran Davtyan says the world medicine has never known before that herbal cells may settle down and parasitize on the organism of a human or an animal. Deeper study of the thorns removed out of the girl's wrist confirmed their vegetative origin. It turned out that the thorns belonged to a cactus that many people had at home.

The only way to save the girl was to perform an operation to remove the fistula to stop the cactus from parasitizing all

[1]http://www.pravdareport.com/health/20-12-2005/9418-mutation-0/

about the organism. The wound healed up after the operation and did not trouble the girl for four years. Narine's mother says the girl could not recover from the shock for a very long period and feared that the thorns might reappear. The tragedy made the girl reserved and unsociable. But still she kept on looking after her pot plants.

One day Narine noticed her wrist turned red once again but she would not confess to her parents that the disease reappeared. The girl felt her forearm swell and soon a thorn as thick as a match burst her skin. This time a fistula appeared in a sinew zone. Narine clenched her fists, the muscles pushed new thorns out and doctors removed them with pincers. At that, the wound was not bleeding. Doctors removed from 70 to 100 thorns from the girl's arm every day. But they still appeared later, which suggested there were two or three parasite cells still staying in the girl's organism. Doctors from many countries stated there was not a surgical but rather a microbiological problem.

When researchers studied the bigger thorns they arrived at a conclusion that they were no longer of vegetative origin. As a result of mutation, the patient got new unknown cells, some sort of a hybrid of a human and a plant. In other words, the young girl was turning into a cactus. Experts believe the terrible metamorphosis sounds warning for mankind. 'Evolution and progress seriously damage the human immune system. People become more vulnerable to unknown parasites and viruses,' Tigran Davtyan says.

Now the girl is 26. When Narine had blood poisoning some people rumored she died. But parents of the girl told doctors Narine was alive but felt too bed. The strange disease made her extremely apathetic and pessimistic as she knows that doctors obviously cannot help her.

(Exchange recorded by local doctor on a house visit; Penilee, Glasgow, Scotland.)

She'd been bedridden for three years and two months when it started. With the drugs she was on, which included sodium amytal, so addictive it's no longer prescribed, strong sunlight hurt her eyes. But she was afraid of total darkness so she lay with the blinds down and the bedside lamp on, day and night. So she didn't really distinguish one from the other, and called for help or comfort at all hours. She got her children and her grandchildren mixed up too, so she had little idea of what decade she was in or how old she was. And yet when the thing took hold she had the same response as people who are completely lucid: embarrassment or shame.

I don't know if this has been followed up. The nearest I've seen to it is the existential disgust that accompanies infestations such as amoebic dysentery. It's a visceral signal to the brain that central control has been violated.

Is that a fact. She didn't want to see a doctor but she agreed to talk to the priest; she was sprouting geraniums in her arms. I would damp them with a sponge. At a certain stage you don't know who you're helping: rooting out the plant can cause shock, neglecting it can lead to gangrene, and tending it means its host will eventually be overcome. But then it's all that's left of your dear one, and you don't want it to die. When your mother stops responding and then stops breathing, it's her. Ultimately there was no difficult decision for us: geraniums don't survive the winter in this climate, and we have a little sun porch at the back of the house, so we installed her there, in one of those long clay pots the undertakers have started marketing, and that's that. In a way I must say I feel she's still with us, but at peace now. Of course it's not so easy if you live in a high-rise, without even a window box, and getting a heavy plant down ten flights of steps and into the park costs money if you don't have help. And then where do you plant it? People think these things are particularly infectious – it's not been our experience, but there we are.

In June the government shut down most of the poultry farms in central France; the places were cruel and filthy but that's not why they were closed. I was the cameraman employed by a group of animal rights activists to document the state of poultry in a large battery farm near Bresse. They had tried to talk their way into another one, which not only refused them entry but electrified its boundary fence and brought in a security firm to guard it. The one we targeted after that had a somewhat neglected look about it, which didn't prepare us for the criminal neglect we found inside. I was led in through a break in the fence by a couple of monosyllabic anarchists who kept watch while I did the business; it took two hours, in the middle of the night, of course. Not that the hangar had any natural light anyway. The place stank, but not like a farmyard – the nose gets used to manure within a few minutes; this was something else, parts-per-million that kept jangling receptors with signals my brain didn't know where to put. Notes of chemistry lab and advanced decomposition. That would be the dead chickens we found pecked and trampled flat by others; eggs crawling with lice, swarms of maggots on the floor picking through detritus and presumably responsible in part at least for the pitiful aspect of the living birds in the wire traps above, many thousands of them, each enclosure grossly overcrowded.

We got out undetected and edited a punchy little video that we sent to the press, which wouldn't air it. So we hoisted it on the net and waited for the supermarket lawyers to bite back, which took just a few hours. There was a public outcry and really vigorous damage control: rogue establishment, major employer, potential job losses; irreplaceable source of nutrition (there they had a point: factory fish and poultry were all the people trusted by that stage). The government had taken control of the issue and everything would be fine; emergency legislation was prepared to reassure the public, then suddenly a hundred poultry breeders got shut down, as did the whole story. Here's why.

During the government fight-back my animal rights employers decided to go for more evidence, so they found another slovenly business to infiltrate. Same routine. 2 a.m. bolt cutters on the back gate, one of the hoodies gets in through an air vent and opens the door for me (not that it had been locked). Same u.v. pilot lights but this was different. It's like you go into a bar in a strange little town – a really strange one – and everyone stops and turns to stare at you. There was no one but me in the shed, so I was the object of attention, which was silly, was it not? So I got to work, I started filming. Pitcher plants. I don't know if you've ever seen them or more to the point been in their company. You could try the Jardin des Plantes if it weren't off limits, or perhaps Kew Gardens. Kew has a little separate room for them, dank and warm. They're basically pitchers of gastric juice, open to the air, some giving off an attractive hint of carrion, for the flies they eat. And the mice. And on occasion rats.

And in this 2 a.m. hangar of mine – very, very many specimens of *Gallus gallus domesticus*. And somehow or other, I believe, the worker who had come to distribute feed or gauge the water or whatever, a number of days before. I stopped filming. I stopped breathing and very nearly didn't start again, fifty metres from the door down a narrow corridor overhung with several thousand grossly distended, salivating pitcher plants. Of course they weren't going to jump on me, but why don't *you* try to be rational in that situation. They brushed against me as I made my way between them to the exit. Then I suggested to my hoodie colleague that we shut the door behind us, hang the padlock on the gate and drive far away.

Now, this had to be reported, but to whom? Not the police who would arrest us for breaking and entering. Not the food and agriculture department that was busy covering up the conventional poultry scandal. Not the press, which hadn't responded last time. Not the health authorities, who would want me quarantined. Since they didn't have any treatment to propose, I wasn't for that.

There was an army barracks not far off. I got its address and enquiries number from the front gate then I went to the nearest accident and emergency department. Told them someone at the farm, too sick to call, had asked me to notify them. Told them I'd lost my mobile and asked if I could make a local call. Called the barracks, told them there was a huge outbreak of SEPS at that poultry farm, and rang off. Then I did my best to disappear.

Watching TV not two days later I learned that the government had done a U-turn and had locked down all the poultry farms in the region. Driving past the pitcher plant gathering, I saw it had acquired a barbed-wire fence, army guards (some speaking English) and inside that a cordon sanitaire and people in full protective suits.

That's a funny thing about SEPS: people can get almost sentimental about it. They think their loved ones have been transformed and are still with them. It's maybe true in some cases, but if they turn into a carnivorous plant, it's fair to assume that their attitude to human and other animals gets transformed too.

From early on it was noted that SEPS infected domestic animals, not wild ones. What we're seeing is a return to the wild.

After the vote, as new ministers wiped their knives and wondered whether to go for continental Brexit or full English Brexit, graduate students of law and public health in brick and bicycle cafés got set to challenge the referendum result on the grounds that the 'leave' campaign had associated SEPS with immigration and a 'leave' vote with containment strategy. Which was quite irrelevant: the 'leave' campaign's US adviser knew that facts don't work or matter – something facts have in common with a swathe of 'leave' voters, people abandoned to their fates and their estates, with their parents and children, by Her Majesty's Government and its loyal opposition. The winner had intended to lose and then feign disappointment; his opponent didn't pretend he was sorry to lose. So why campaign? There are known unknowns and unknown unknowns, and there are worse things to worry about, such as SEPS.

Even stupid people aren't stupid. When the BBC announces, a propos of nothing, that medical examinations don't cause SEPS, they understand it's better to avoid them. When they learn that business leaders have retreated to their enclaves and that no one is physically present anymore at Prime Minister's question time, they understand that they've been abandoned once again.

The poor have their own enclaves. Take housing scheme P, just north of city G, which had become a centre of excellence in vehicle management, for recreation more than trade: vacant lots were dotted with burned-out wrecks. The police had responded by building a fence round the whole area, leaving only one way in and one way out for road traffic. The scheme itself was a food desert with almost no fresh deliveries to the corner shops, just packets and tins. From the days of video vans through satellite TV to mobile apps, residents had grown accustomed to seeking face-to-face contact with just about no one outside their house or indeed their bedroom. SEPS changed that.

Casually at first, the two gaps in the fence were watched by residents. Delivery vans were checked for fresh fruit and veg.. Itinerant vendors of crystals and powders were cleared, but weed was no longer welcome. These decisions, more or less tacit, were uncontroversial, but they weren't seen as sufficient, so community representatives (those who could tear themselves away from their screens) met to discuss things, one fine evening, in the children's playground.

These were more or less exclusively 'leave' voters, by which they meant that Cameron should leave, Johnson should leave, Britain should leave, Europe should leave; anyone who wasn't going to help them should leave them alone. If they had voted they would have voted 'leave'.

It turns out that variants of this scenario, a po-mo Parliament of St Kilda, had replicated at a thousand points in the United Kingdom of Great Britain and Northern Ireland. It was all about containment and it boiled down to three lines of argument (in various permutations): right, left and providential.

The right wanted to keep outsiders out of the housing scheme, meaning anyone they didn't know. The anarchist left wanted to keep the government out, by restricting or eliminating electronic surveillance and control, everything from CCTV to ultrasound. Others mapped their faith base against the spread of the pandemic and drew conclusions insufferable or compassionate.

The result, within a month, was fairly stark. Except in rare cases where community violence triggered a response from security forces, each side made concessions to the other, with the result that central government awareness of the thoughts and indeed the whereabouts of its citizens was reduced to levels not seen since the 1960s. Government could control and manipulate xenophobic outbursts, which were of necessity public, but neighbourhood watch had nurtured new political configurations, each in its way intent on dealing with SEPS, most avoiding the information superhighway, and none affiliated to any mainstream party, whose members by and large were not welcome in the playground.

Given this situation the conference is asked to consider whether a SEPS containment strategy is feasible or advisable, and how its conclusions might be communicated or put into practice.

I've been thinking, as I lie around chewing my parsley, about survival of the fittest. He hasn't survived, or if he has he's gone strangely quiet. And remembering how we used to all be glued to our little screens. Even when walking along the street, never looking up, bumping into each other like zombie dodgems. Even pedaling our bikes. It's all about closed systems – or is THAT just a side-effect of *Cannabis sativa?* Because he chose cannabis. I chose parsley, mainly for the vitamin C. and opted for hunter-gathering after the district got immured. Not bad: a greenhouse on the roof of an abandoned paper-mill. Some dead bamboo on the fire-escape to frighten folk away. Just the two of us, waiting for it to happen. First sign for me was my period stopped and I certainly wasn't pregnant. First sign for him was this big green stem coming straight out of his chest. Which was not so good: rooted in among the major organs. Not my case. At first you can still go around foraging for stuff, food and drink, bits and pieces. But then you don't really want to and then you really don't want to and then you start snacking on yourself. Which is quite disgusting at first. But then so is the booze. And there's people who drink their own urine, who reckon it's good for them. Beats me. After a bit it's ok and the fact that this particular plant is rooted in you is like a type of grape in a particular soil. Whatever the French say it's the grape that tastes of grape, not the dirt. And as long as you keep moving there's no fixed root. Whenever you wake up you have to tend yourself, prune away any wayward tendrils. But parsley – I didn't know it then – has a strong tap root and in the long run it gets its way, and you're stuck. So here I am wasting away, high as a kite on cannabis fumes (there's no need to smoke it), thinking.

I think therefore I am. I read somewhere that that's a disguised tautology. What it comes down to is I think therefore I think I am, and that can be reduced to I think therefore I think. Which means that the famous link between thinking and being isn't there or isn't that. And survival of the fittest: same routine from the other side of the divide. It's shorthand for survival of the fittest to survive, and that means nothing more than survival of the survivors. One more tautology in fancy dress. Fitness is irrelevant; stuff just happens, and stuff has nothing to do with values, goals and purposes.

Why do I not believe that? Because a system that's really closed, me snacking on my own parsley, can't survive. But now that I've put down roots I'm a completely different proposition and something of that goes on, though not as me. It's not so bad. The economy finds its roots in the environment; politicians have to deal with the unwashed, and science? Science doesn't allow loose talk about intent in cells and genes, but it never stops. 'Just a manner of speaking', which is just a manner of thinking. And however embarrassing they find it, they mustn't stop. They have to keep looking up from their little screens.

If I'm going to the bother of writing this it's because I'm betting it will be read. I'll put it in a bottle and fling it out the window. But the quarantine wall? No problem: given the state of the planet, government is so corrupt that the contract for the wall will have gone to some incompetent. It won't stay up for long.

SEPS is not a disease but a condition or set of conditions that changes the status of its host. Just how profound those changes are we do not yet know, but we seem to be witnessing or experiencing the emergence of a new species, a hybrid that combines human and autotroph intelligence and sensitivity, a species that, if allowed to develop, might be able, by its very existence, to have humanity coexist with the biosphere at the individual and global levels, a marriage that was beginning to seem unviable.

SEPS can and does cause sudden death of the human host, but that is only one of the possible outcomes. Many people are unaffected by it and many hosts have found a modus vivendi that ranges from the painful to the inspiring, often both by turns, rather like conventional human relationships.

Viable and living groups and communities of green people have arisen wherever SEPS has appeared. Those whose condition permits do the active work and tend to those that cannot. People who have succumbed to SEPS are not, in our view, dead. Plants have always communicated whether through yeasts among root systems or by diffusion of volatile compounds in the atmosphere. Active community members try to 'listen' to the aerial messaging, and some success has been reported, though the prevailing view is that we may communicate either verbally or chemically but not both. As always, learning a new language takes time, and since there are no teachers yet, this apprenticeship will not be quick. What we ask for, then, is time and space commensurate with our needs.

State policy, in such States as have survived, tends to be one of quarantine and/or cremation. We demand that cremation cease forthwith. In exchange we undertake to police the boundaries of quarantine areas, letting no one with SEPS encroach on other land.

In a second phase the location and extent of the quarantine must be agreed. There can be no question of refugee camps for us. Nor should we be restricted to homelands, national parks or reservations. Territory must be divided on a per capita basis.

Meeting Report

(a) The relationship between humans and plants since the beginning

Dr Peters put the SEPS epidemic in context, prefacing his observations with the three main points:

1. Plants were here before us;
2. We cannot live without them;
3. They will outlast us.

440 million year ago plants (reproducing through spores) appeared on land. Plants had cooperated with other groups: lichens (a symbiosis of algae and fungi), and mycorrhiza (fungal roots), which enhanced nutrient uptake, helping plants to develop on land, where they developed cuticle and vascular tissue. 408 million years ago vascular plants diversified and grew bigger.

362 million years ago, there were gymnosperms with naked ovaries and unprotected seeds. 323 million years ago the system was more complex; abundant plants produced oxygen and organic material, which affected the global climate. Plant communities evolved that traded nutrients. The forest prevailed. 130 million years ago flowering plants such as magnolia came into being, pollinated by beetles; plants' ovaries were now protected from the clumsy insects. Animals were needed to disperse the protected seeds; plants developed attractive fruit, which the animals duly consumed and dispersed. Throughout that time, plants evolved in response to local environmental conditions, which were changed by the encroaching vegetation.

Fast forward to 3.9 million years ago, and the appearance of the *Australopithecus* genus of hominid. 2.4 million years ago was the era of *Homo habilis* and the first evidence of stone tools. 1.7 million years ago *Homo erectus*, who used fire and complex tools, migrated from Africa. 0.3 – 0.4 million years ago we find *Homo heidelbergensis* and *Homo neanderthalensis*. 195 000 years ago – *Homo sapiens*. 28 000 years ago, the other hominids have disappeared from the fossil record. 20 000 years ago dogs are domesticated.

Hunter-gatherers had healthy diets, they exercised and had a good balance with the environment. 12 000 years ago the agricultural revolution introduced the division of labour, hierarchy, trade, ownership, and a high density of people staying in one place, which helped spread disease. Before the agricultural revolution 7 000 species of plants were used, while today only thirty crops provide 95% of human food energy needs; rice, wheat, maize and potatoes provide 60% of our energy intake. 75% of plant genetic diversity has been lost since the agricultural revolution. 70% of existing plants risk being lost.

The impact of human beings on the life of plants could be summarized as follows:
Habitat loss: seventy per cent of plants and animals live in forests. Ninety per cent of forest cover has been removed in the USA in the last four centuries.
Global climate change: the earth is warming (each year since the millennium has been the warmest on record); the seas are warming and becoming more acidic; precipitation, wind patterns and extreme weather events are becoming more frequent and less regular, which makes it hard for plants to adapt.
Loss of soil and reduction of fertility: half of the topsoil on the planet has been lost in the last 150 years, and the release of carbon from soils increases climate change.
Loss of pollinators and dispersers: most plants are pollinated or dispersed by animals and insects, which are being killed by pesticides and climate change.

With that, Dr Peters returned to the third of his initial points: plants will survive humanity, since they are very clever in reproducing their genotype. They adapt to climates where humans cannot live, such as the Atacama Desert in Chile, which has no rainfall. If, as would appear, plants have mutated in such a way as to draw nutrients from the source of their distress, then that mutation will have an immense selective advantage. SEPS might therefore be a turning point.

It was pointed out that domesticated corn would not survive if humans were to disappear; wild species, on the other hand, did not need humans. Forests would return to what was loosely termed their natural state.

(b) *The relationship between humans and plants in urban settlements*

Of course, since the agricultural revolution, the nature of Nature has become a conundrum – on which more in section 4, below. Turning from the evolutionary timeline to recorded history, Ms Borelli deployed a sequence of images to show how human society, initially encysted in the natural world, came to incorporate the plant kingdom, reducing primeval forest to a number of enclosures and reservations, and reducing species to distorted specimens. In a similarly twisted way, the drive to control nature implies a kind of veneration. For humans, the colour green is emblematic of the plant kingdom, and is precious in itself; green is balance, refreshment and peace. Greenery means water and life – and higher real-estate values. The original sense of the word 'paradise' was 'walled garden'. Indeed, the word 'garden' retains the notion of 'guard', to keep us in and them out, or vice versa. To monopolize enjoyment.

The modern focus of this confrontation is the city, habitat of most of humanity. Here – perhaps like early hominids in the forest – plants are not entirely welcome. They are cultivated in parks, gardens, courtyards, terraces and pots, and worked as single crops in vast hinterlands. Even natural seeding is supplanted by industrial seeding. Deprived of their own territory, plants are made to define boundaries in urban settlements. They are paraded as cut flowers, topiaries and bonsai.

For all this, as soon as human control slips, the plant kingdom is quick to reassert itself. We see this in every poppy that grows between cobblestones, in the fireweed that graces burned-out tenements, and in entire geographical areas, such as the Demilitarized Zone (DMZ), Chernobyl, narcotrafficking corridors and – in one sense – the corn belt of the United States.

The DMZ separates the two Koreas at the 38th parallel. Innumerable landmines, fortified barriers and watchtowers have kept it human-free since 1953. Forests, wetlands and estuaries luxuriate; the Asian black bear has nothing to fear but tripwires. Seventy mammals, 320 kinds of birds and 3000 plant species show what is possible when Nature sets the balance. Is war a prerequisite for the reinstatement of paradise on earth?

The Chernobyl disaster of 1986 resulted in uncounted deaths during and immediately after the meltdown of the reactor. Thousands would die of exposure to radiation in the medium term, and hundreds of thousands risk cancer and acute radiation syndrome thereafter. Some 350,000 people were evacuated from the vicinity, though a few hundred chose to remain in the Zone, within 30 kilometres of the stricken reactor. Some estimate that the area will not be safe for human life for another 20,000 years. The Zone, like the DMZ, has reverted to Nature, which is resetting the balance.

In the narco-trafficking corridors of Asia and South America opium and coca leaf are intensively cultivated but other crops are not, and human settlements are scarce. Plants and animals all thrive in these zones. Once again, Nature has built on human destruction.

In a rather different register, Nature has proved capable of its own brand of destructive monoculture, though once again this has resulted from human miscalculation. Kuzdu is a perennial vine originating from Asia that can spread at the rate of 150 000 acres per year. In 1935, as dust storms ravaged the prairies, the Soil Conservation Service planted more than seventy million kudzu seedlings to prevent erosion, and the United States government paid anyone willing to plant the vine, which was marketed as a high-protein feed for cattle. Some 1.2 million hectares of kudzu were planted. By 1945 it was rendering farms unviable; in 1970 it was registered as a weed, and in 1997 as a noxious weed. It is said to cover up to nine million acres across the southern USA, and it is still advancing over land, power lines and buildings.

In human societies, oppression can lead to reaction (see part 6, below). Might the Kudzu invasion be a natural response to the human monocultures of genetically-modified corn and soy? Can SEPS be viewed in a similar way? Each case of SEPS encapsulates the dichotomy between the human universe and the natural universe. The outbreak is an additional episode in the history of the human/plant relationship, and one by which humans are pressed into judgement or action when a breaking point occurs. Wilful ignorance, human greed and unbridled addictions have left humans illiterate in the language of plants, unknowing of Nature's ways. How can this be remedied? Though human species and plants do not share the same language, some humans devote themselves to communicating and even accommodating plant needs, as evidenced by the establishment of conservation areas, nurseries, and individual and community gardens. Might they mediate? Could any of the people who have contracted SEPS interpret between plant and human kingdoms in some way? Because what we have, in the SEPS epidemic, is a more aggressive push for plants to sustain themselves.

The epidemiologist provided an update and overview on the initial appearance and reporting of SEPS.

Since detection of the first case of SEPS, it is surmised that the disease started in January of this year. The outbreak emerged on every continent in seeming synchronicity; it did not spread from one place to another. Thus far, SEPS has affected 30% of the population in areas where it appeared; 50% of those affected have died. More than half of the survivors are left with serious disabilities, resulting in limited mobility or ability to care for themselves.

We have no idea of what is happening. We can only look at patterns. Plant species are taking up residence in the human body.

The transmission pathway is a matter of speculation. Had we been faced with human infestation by a single species of plant, it would have been possible to look for a mutation in that plant, and subsequently, ways of blocking it.

However, we are dealing with a paradigm shift in an indefinite number of species. Mechanisms must be studied, as they have not been examined in sufficient depth to help us. The quagmire to resolve is communication between plants of different species. This can be either atmospheric or chthonic. We know that sage, when attacked by caterpillars, secretes higher levels of tannins to repel the grubs. At the same time, it releases compounds such as methyl jasmonate, which prompts neighbouring plants to increase the tannin levels in their foliage, in order to repel the same predators. Chthonic communication between plants would seem to involve yeasts that act as messengers between the root systems of trees and other autotrophs.

Our assumption, which is no more than that at this stage, is that the much more complex change in autotroph feeding patterns is triggered by a similar type of communication. If this is so, then we can see the postman, but we have no idea of the contents of the letter.

The speed of SEPS infection or growth may also be a function of the attacking plants' life cycle (for example: mushrooms can appear overnight; fungi and ivy are much faster growing than redwood).

SEPS is thought to be associated with a specific form of microbial gut flora (microbiota). There are more than 1000 different bacterial species found in the human gut, yet only around 150 predominate in any given subject. Microbiota types are based on diversity and dominance of different bacterial species. Different types of bacteria can be found in different parts of the gut. Examination of the types, from a technical standpoint, will be arduous and time-consuming. At a population level, knowledge is extremely sparse.

Most authorities agree that there are four main types of microbiota, with 3-8 sub-types in each. So far, no SEPS has been found in people with Type II microbiota or in Type I Subtype 4 and Type III Subtype 8. Approximately 10% of the population may have protection, although prevalence of microbiota types around the world is unknown. Monkeys in captivity can develop microbiota types that are similar to those of humans (ie much less diverse).

Does SEPS originate from within or without the microbiome?
Microbiome refers to the DNA (genomes) of the microbiota. A wide-scale and thorough study of microbiome could accelerate investigation and understanding of this epidemic.

Four major gut microbiota types in humans with approximate distribution in humans

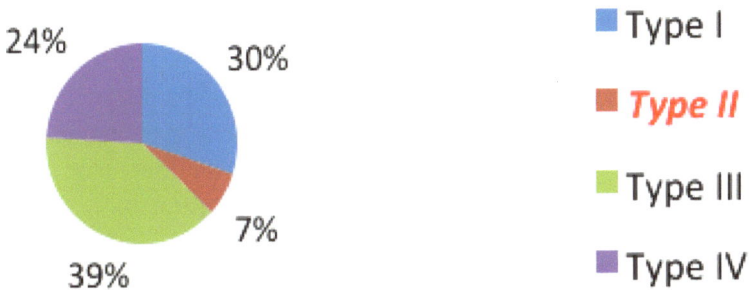

Thus far, no SEPS has been found in microbiota Type II, but this represents only 7% of all types. Type II appears more common in very rural, remote communities. However, data about these communities are limited and the disease might not be recognized as such. (It has even been suggested that some cultures may actually see the invasion of plants as a gift rather than a disease). It is not clear whether people with SEPS have a specific type of microbiota or whether SEPS modifies the microbiota. One possibility is to study people with a specific type of microbiota and determine if they are susceptible to SEPS.

The connection between gut bacteria and SEPS is founded on the hypothesis that at the start of the outbreak, an imbalance in microbiome allowed plants to reside in the human body. Microbiota, like plants, have evolved over long periods of time and evolution. Some other change, climatic or otherwise, may have prompted this epidemic. Something may also have changed dramatically in the environment—unbeknownst to or ignored by humans—that triggered rapid progression of the disease. Antimicrobial resistance may also be a factor in the propagation of SEPS.

As people, especially travellers, know all too well, the flora in human stomachs is an ecosystem. Gut flora is very effective in getting rid of an invader, and a possible connection with diet ought to be explored. Some bacteria in the gut assist in the production of enzymes and vitamins. Plants growing in the gut may spur chemical reactions that are distinct from mechanical effects (plants affecting circulation, the function of other organs, etc.). Could this be a milestone case of symbiosis between bacteria and intestinal flora?

The issue of a connection to parasites has been raised. Parasites harm the host. For instance, schistosomiasis results in calcification and fibrosis of the liver. The parasite can also kill its host, and it will not survive without it, as in the case of malaria. *Plasmodium vivax* does not kill its host and may reappear years after the first occurrence of the disease. *Plasmodium falciparum* can kill its host in a few days and then die.

It is not known whether SEPS plants can survive without the human body. The attacking plants may very well be benefitting from the host. Plants adapting to the new environment might develop into a new species. In people with long-term SEPS, these plants may evolve into a completely different species. An autopsy of the human body could help determine whether plants use the vascular system of the host. Just as seeds can sprout in the dark waiting for light to develop (no photosynthesis is required), the plants may have built-in mechanisms to survive the host.

It is not certain pollen can spread the disease, although it does transit through the human body. For example, it is present in the mucus smear of tuberculosis patients, but does not affect it. Pollen has half the genetic material; the seed is needed if the plant is to grow. Some seeds are eaten, but not digested.

Evolution has created situations where seeds are dispersed through the human body.

It is not surprising that plants are present in the human body. What is surprising is the form that they are taking.

Bio-terrorism is unlikely: SEPS is indiscriminate and does not seem to have a target, or a perpetrator.

Reporting of infection

Reporting of the disease and data collection during February and March was patchy. Following a warning issued by the Centers for Disease Control in May, more cases were reported. From June onwards, an increasing number of cases, ranging from 300 to 1000, were reported each month. In the past month, reported cases have levelled off. Is this due to underreporting or has the appearance of the disease truly plateaued, suggesting a kind of balance?

It is too early to say. Epidemics move in waves: there is a surge, some survive, the number of people reaches a tipping point, and equilibrium is achieved. The proportion of people susceptible to the disease increases in the absence of it.

Most epidemiologists surmise that the levelling is due to underreporting. A level of fear has gained traction; people are fleeing urban areas, and health workers are leaving health centres. We do not have enough information. The infrastructure that usually provides data is not working. The link with microbiota types is purely theoretical, and we are far from finding what the definite causative agent is. Evidence of increased exposure to electromagnetic energy has been anecdotally documented, though is yet to be substantiated.

If indeed there is underreporting, the disease is likely to spread fast and could result in a swell of cases by the end of the year, reaching as high as 18 million.

In most epidemics, there is only one pathogen. With SEPS, there are many plant species. The question is mutation. This infection is not following the usual pattern. There is no common source of infection. SEPS is spreading sporadically and simultaneously in different parts of the world. The plant species attacking the microbiota need a catalyst. That catalyst is the unknown factor.

3.   *Vulnerable Groups*

Dr. Jesus Ramirez-Valles observed that SEPS, thus far, has been understood as a plant-centric phenomenon. There is latent belief that a movement of plant retaliation is underway, a reaction to centuries of human misrule, the system's method of correcting the equilibrium.

In the meantime, humans are being stigmatized because plants are coming out of them. Who are we going to save? The plants or ourselves? What are the possibilities of saving anybody?

It appears that wild animals may be less at risk. Yet, the risk that is posed by domestic animals and zoo animals has not been fully considered. Do those creatures carry the disease? It is possible that those in isolated areas remain untouched, or that caged animals are infected and we do not know it. How close should humans get to them?

Humans also have close and constant proximity to their pets and domestic animals. Domestic animals are more susceptible to the epidemic than those in the wild. Again, the closeness of contact implies rapid transmission of the disease. How much effort should be deployed in saving them? They are living animals that share the closest proximity to their human guardians. In many cases they are considered members of the family, particularly for the upper classes. If a pussycat begins sprouting branches, what is the danger it represents? Should we care? The animals living in closest contact with us will be the ones most at risk. Due to the reduced use of cellphones and computers, it will be difficult to communicate with people in a similar situation and to keep track of this cohort during the epidemic.

The most vulnerable humans are those with the fewest resources, and situated on the margins of the mainstream. The vulnerable are the poor, the elderly, immigrants and those who are not heterosexual or not white. How will these groups be protected? SEPS is a condition that leads to stigmatization. Those vulnerable groups will be even more stigmatized by SEPS.

The issue to confront is how to protect people who are marginalized by their own societies. They are already lacking basic resources such as food, shelter, access to health care and education, and these groups will likely be slow to even realize what is happening before being forced to grapple with the sudden emergence of a public health crisis, controlled by groups located elsewhere. There will be confusion, particularly during the early stages of communication campaigns. It is certain there will be difficulty in understanding what is happening at the beginning of the epidemic with any clarity or lucidity. People will have to be familiarized with the condition and provided with information on how the disease spreads.

The groups in question are defined more by their social class than by any other marker of identity or category. More likely than not, they are poor because their societies have deprived them of resources, on the premise of their lower social status and limited potential. Vulnerable groups are ones that are frequently defined by their skin colour, their supposedly defective genes, deteriorated bodies, limited mental abilities, and an inability (or excessive propensity) to reproduce.

SEPS signals yet another return to an old concept: stigma, the negative mark stamped on individuals and groups through the construction of the label and attribution of it. In the case of SEPS, it is a condition that causes physical distortion, wilting, dryness. Stigma will result from the physical characteristics of the disease and the carrier. This condition deforms the human body. Since the causes and the consequences are unknown, people will be consumed with fear. Those carrying the disease will be feared and assumed to be dangerous. Health care providers, family members, neighbours, employers, schoolteachers and likely all members of the larger society will treat carriers with intense trepidation.

Groups that are currently in vulnerable social positions and are stigmatized are certain to be even further stigmatized once they are confirmed to be infected. We will have a case of layered stigma. Increased marginalization will occur, along with a strong possibility of increased mortality, morbidity, and social unrest.

On the one hand, there could be a systemic effect. The decrepit conditions—social, physical, financial and educational—are already in place. This provides fertile ground for an added condition of marginalization to take hold and amplify. Social consequences and heightened stigma will be all but guaranteed.

On the other hand, there are the possibilities stemming from the social reaction to the condition, and to vulnerable groups. The powers that be will call for quarantines; there may be a proliferation of asylums to keep the sick away for the rest of society. Again, those most likely to be affected are the poor, the elderly, black people, immigrants, women, and queers. One can imagine this entire swathe of the population being subjected to a form of institutional stigma.

Stigma can be considered an irony, seen through the argument that plants are a positive force, a symbol of something enlightened, as Ms Borelli has explained. Humans in the past have manifested a love and reverence for plants. Yet when plants are the ones causing havoc from within, generating chaos without, demonstrating power, control or ability to manipulate, humans become stigmatized.

In the case of HIV and AIDS, humans played a major role in spreading the epidemic. First by socio-economic factors that created migrations, changes in ways of living, and commercialization of blood. Then, the silence of governments and their negative views of non-white populations, gay men, drug users, and sex workers, slowed down any response to control the epidemic or care for those affected. How can SEPS be understood through the lens of that experience? What examples or tendencies shown during that epidemic are to be repeated, avoided, altered?

SEPS will exacerbate the social, economic, and political disparities that were systemic pre-SEPS and will create increased pressure on those same groups. Their social standing will be further eroded and made fragile. Those in power will call for quarantine. Those most vulnerable will be further isolated. Any protection conferred on them could only result from deliberate allocation of resources, already strained and subject to intense competition. Any effort to protect those groups could only result from an act of collective and political will.

The crucial question emerges: what do we value and how can we save it? Who among humans ought to survive and therefore be protected? Whose pain will warrant relief over that of others? The answers are already apparent in how some vulnerable groups are faring. The position society has taken in dealing with the marginalized is manifest in everyday examples (such as migration, poor working conditions, and lack of access to health care). It is simply hoisted to the surface during as critical and dramatic an epidemic as SEPS.

Tremendous resources will be needed to protect and treat the vulnerable from SEPS, and from the reaction of society as a whole. Why? Vulnerable groups are no longer viewed as fellow humans with simply fewer resources. They will be viewed as rebels and perpetrators of social unrest. History shows that poverty, man-made and natural disasters have led to social disruption. People will compete for scarce resources, and through vengeance and greed, take justice into their own hands. This has been averted thus far in the case of SEPS. Yet if the rate of infection continues unmitigated, in tandem with low levels of pro-activeness, war may be on the horizon.

4. *Conflicting Priorities*

Health of people (medicine), of populations (public health), of the ecosystem (ecology) and of life (biology as opposed to entropy).

Professor Maclean pointed out that, throughout human history, the interaction between humans and plants has inspired fascination. The work of the Italian painter Giuseppe Arcimboldo is an apt encapsulation of both the lived and imagined experience with nature. In and of itself, this art is natural.

A portrait of a man, whose constitution is defined by an array of fruits, vegetables, plants and tree roots. Whimsical at first blush, yet logical—natural—when considering the anatomical shapes of the human body and their correspondence to the individual objects chosen. The alignments in shapes and objects suggest that there is nothing random in such a composition.

The name of the painting, Vertumnus, is the Roman god of metamorphoses in life and in nature. The fruits and vegetables symbolize the abundance of the Golden Age that returned to Prague under Emperor Rudolf II. Clearly, symbiosis between humans and nature has been fathomed in art. Is such symbiosis now finding expression in SEPS?

History is replete with episodes of fear and hope generated by humans as they test the thresholds of interaction with nature.

(1) Nuclear fear: throughout the 1930s, in all manner of media, books, comics and films, there were traces of an ambivalent attitude to nuclear power even before nuclear fission.
(2) Reactions to scientists tinkering with the human gene even before the technology was developed. Sources of reactions are much deeper.

Art, in its foretelling way, outlined the dilemma that SEPS poses today. In the 1950s film *The Invasion of The Body Snatchers*, humans were being replaced by duplicates from outer space. Spores that fell from space grew into pods, to replicate any person found in close proximity—not unlike SEPS' discreet and random transmission. A quiet invasion begins, as the pods replicate into 'emotionless' humans, devoid of all feeling. The pods not only take on the physical attributes of the human subjects, they assimilate the memories, the characters, the personalities, which individually define each person. Humans were not only being overtaken by something foreign, but their very identity as emotional or sentient beings undergoes alteration. Is the process one of deformation or reformation? The question has been posed before.

As the film shows, the entire ecosystem of the human body is pressed into service during a foreign invasion. Scientists suggest that SEPS must be investigated as originating from the gut. We should not only focus on intestinal flora, but also look at other body functions. Examining microbiota is the logical starting point, rendered all the more imperative when recognizing that 2-6 pounds of body weight is made up of microbiota, a system supported by other systems within the body.

The boundary of an organism begins to expand if we think of it in terms of *ecosystems*. The body cannot be thought of as a fortress.

How do we frame the problem before us? It all begins with nature.

Attempting to understand any phenomenon is to choose (subjectively) a method to frame the question, and to accept the subjectivities that stem from that decision. How can SEPS be understood? It is either (1) a case of plants invading humans, or (2) a case of humans turning into plants. The ethical implications will be different, hinging entirely on how the case is framed.

If plants are invading humans, taking up residence in the body, sprouting and multiplying from the human host, humans are likely to seek to destroy the plants, or cure themselves. The philosopher John Broome would say that plants are attacking us. The poet Meng Chiao (see document 6, Cultural Precedents) would disagree.

If humans are turning into plants, the process could be reversed. Humans could even be returning to their primordial state. SEPS is not a condition or a disease, but an evolutionary occurrence. Defining something as a disease is anthropocentric. It is possible we are part of a flow. The plants could be regarded as successors and therefore would be treated very differently, perhaps with some respect. In this scenario, the process of turning into plants would be considered *natural*: a concept that strikes at the core of the human relationship with nature, not least at the meaning of nature itself.

How we understand our relationship with nature is best undertaken by thinking about what we are contrasting the meaning of nature to. In the eighteenth century, the philosopher David Hume addressed the question of the human relationship to nature when he considered whether moral goodness was natural and evil unnatural. *'The answer to this question,'* he writes, *'depends upon the definition of the word, Nature, than which there is none more ambiguous and equivocal.'*[2] Hume illustrates the difficulty by listing three different concepts to which nature stands in contrast.

> 1. Nature in contrast to the supernatural. Everything is subject to natural laws, including humans, as part of nature. Nature includes whatever is governed and explained by natural laws or science. Humans are subject to natural laws, and thus humans and everything they do are part of nature. 'If nature be oppos'd to miracles, not only the distinction betwixt vice and virtue is natural, but also every event, which has ever happen'd in the world, excepting those miracles, on which our religion is founded.' (p. 474). This is the view of philosophical naturalists.

> 2. Nature in contrast to the unusual. Humans construct expectations as to what is natural, or the natural order of things. When expectations are met, we consider this to be part of the natural order. When something unusual occurs, for example, people sprouting twigs and thorns from their fingers and wrists, so rare and unfamiliar are such happenings that they would be regarded as 'unnatural' and insensitively called freaks of nature. Hume writes, 'nature may also be opposed to rare and unusual; and in this sense of the word,

---

[2]Hume, David. *A Treatise of Human Nature.* (1739). Oxford University Press, 1967, p. 474.

which is the common one, there may often arise disputes concerning what is natural or unnatural.' (p. 474).

3. Nature in contrast to artifice, or in his words, 'Nature may also be opposed to artifice.' (p. 475) Only what exists without human interference is natural. All human creation—institutions, technologies and art—are not natural. They are interventions into nature, regardless of moral sentiments, which would be artefacts.

This third distinction underpins the early environmental movement in the United States at the turn of the twentieth century to preserve the wilderness and natural environment in its purest state. It is a school of thought associated with naturalist and environmental philosopher John Muir (another Scot), a pioneer of the preservationist movement that led to the Yellowstone Act and the creation of the first national park in 1872. With the development of ecology, humans are seen as part of nature, not in contrast to nature.

The contrast between Hume's first and third senses is at the heart of a question that has a lengthy philosophical history and has been in the background of environmental ethics: are humans part of nature; or are we separate from nature, standing part from and intervening in it?

There are older and deeper senses in which we understand the contrast, going back to the ancients and the philosopher Heraclitus. In around 500BC, Heraclitus deposited a book of epigrams in the temple of Artemis. The book supposedly contained the sum of his knowledge expressed in aphorisms and epigrams, including one of consisting of just three words: *phusis kruptesthai philei*. Philosopher and philologist Pierre Hadot argued that it is impossible to know precisely what Heraclitus intended through this saying. After some 500 years during which Greek language and philosophy evolved significantly, the epigram is now commonly understood as 'Nature loves to hide.' According to him, the movement of understanding and responding to this epigram demonstrates two very different attitudes that Greek, pagan, Judeo-Christian and modern philosophers have taken to nature. These attitudes, conveniently enough, correspond to two of Hume's contrasts to nature.

> 1. Man places himself in opposition to nature and views nature's *hiding of secrets* as an act of resistance. Through technology, control and power, man seeks to dominate his rights over nature.

> 2. Man places himself as part of nature; art is present in nature; there is no opposition between nature and art; human art is a prolongation of nature and therefore there is no relation of dominance between nature and mankind. The occultation of nature will be perceived not as a resistance that must be conquered, but as a mystery into which human beings can be gradually initiated.[3]

If the gods are in nature, art can reveal its secrets. For Hadot (and Hesiod), Prometheus stole the secret of fire to improve the life of mankind, unleashing the benefits of technology and civilization. Orpheus, lyrist and singer, was able to unlock the secrets of nature not through violence, but melody, rhythm and harmony (pp. 95–6). The lesson that humans must draw is that we should marshal the courage to face 'nature's secrets,' decline opposition, and refrain from regarding nature as something alien. Humans ought to engage in what Hadot terms as experimentation with nature. This view became the basis of scientific thought in the Middle Ages. Francis Ba-

---

[3] Hadot, Pierre. *The Veil of Isis.* Harvard University Press, 2006, p. 92.

con, the father of modern science, compares the experimental method to a procedure applied to a hostile witness. He writes, 'The secrets of nature are better revealed under the torture of experiments than when they follow their natural course.' (p. 120). Humans force nature into understanding their questions. One must experiment.

However, that idea means that nature is being subjugated. Bacon and his most famous followers – Newton, Kepler, and Galileo – were scientists for religious reasons. Their actions were part of an endeavor to give humans control over nature, as they believed God had intended. This theme is thoroughly developed by historian Lynn White Jr., who wrote that the marriage of science and technology in Europe after the Enlightenment produced the powerful technologies that have now unleashed 'the problem of ecologic[al] backlash.'[4] Human ecology is fundamentally conditioned by human beliefs about nature and destiny: nothing short of religion. Even when religion, through the attempts of Saint Francis of Assisi, sought to place man as a humble player within nature '…a democracy of all God's creatures…' it failed. Christianity triumphed over paganism in the early Middle Ages. Not long after, Christianity ushered in the repudiation of animism of ancient religions.

It is clear that the prevailing attitude in European and American culture is one in which humans have viewed themselves as separate from nature, and this attitude remains in full force today. In White's words, 'Despite Darwin, we are *not*, in our hearts, part of the natural process. We are superior to nature, contemptuous of it, willing to use it for our slightest whim … what we do about our ecology depends on our ideas of the man-nature relationship. More science and more technology are not going to get us out of the present ecologic crisis until we find a new religion, or rethink our old one.' (p. 1206)

---

[4]White, Jr., Lynn. 'The Historic Roots of Our Ecologic Crisis,' *Science* 155, no. 3767 (1967): 1203-1207.

The advent of SEPS compels a broad question: is SEPS a disease, wherein man chooses to lock himself in opposition against nature? This epidemic is different from others, however. Those who are used to dodging previous crises cannot avoid it now.

It might not be an entirely bad thing if plants push humans away, but people do not want to die. The dilemma is that we have the means to do things, but lack the wisdom to deal with the problem. Other epidemics, such as polio and HIV, have been equally unusual to the same degree. The problem of prioritizing remains unresolved. As John Broome articulates in the book *Weighing Lives*, we are faced with decisions that require us to weigh lives against other lives or lives against other things. We are obliged to make both quantitative and qualitative choices. Decisions are paramount to a cost-benefit analysis, leading to determining the economic value of human life, translated by the monetary value of human life and ultimately discounting the value of life, further attenuated by the cost of prolonging life (through health insurance).

Is SEPS an invitation to a conceptual revolution? To save ourselves, to move beyond the loops of centuries' history of philosophical questions on our relationship to nature, could we be on the verge of reintroducing animism, one of the oldest belief systems in the world, founded on the 'supernatural'? Would we be better served by subscribing to a system that sees no separation between the spiritual and physical world, in our perspective of nature?

Ambassador Rapp broached a number of legal issues that would frame any understanding of and response to Severe Epidemic Phytonotic Syndrome (SEPS).

Who can be held legally responsible for the epidemic and how do we pay for its effect on society? In confronting SEPS, the law intervenes at two levels: firstly, where and how human life is defined; secondly, where and how the State may act, with a view to protecting human life.

One must firstly consider a separation between human rights and plant rights.

The starting point begins as a very human issue. Grandma is sitting peacefully in her parlour and one day begins sprouting leaves. At what point does she cease being a human and become a plant? When does life start, when does it end? How do we determine its end point before her human status is supplanted by her condition as an autotroph? If and when she becomes a plant, what are her rights? Do plants even have rights?

While this will come as a shock to some, it is abundantly clear that under the law, only humans have rights. Humans are free to do whatever they please to plants without concern for their welfare.

As this field of law emerges, we may anticipate likening the issue to animal rights, which were forged, fought and fostered by animal lovers who care as much or more about their animals as they do about their neighbours' views on their animals (to assume the very least) or care more about their animals than about their neighbours. There are laws preventing cruelty to animals. Animals do not have political or civil rights; their legal protection is conferred to protect their protectors from the anguish that stems from any suffering their animals could succumb to. At the end of the day, humans can do as they wish with animals. The latter do not have rights.

To return to the preceding question then, when does grandma cease to be human? The definition boils down to the essential factors of human viability: a heartbeat, a breath, a brain function.

In the United States, as in many other jurisdictions, when an embryo is unable to survive outside the mother, the law no longer views such entity as human life. Some argue that life begins at the point of conception. This is not recognized internationally.

When a human body can no longer sustain a breath or a heartbeat, society as a whole is under no obligation to provide resuscitation. Doctors, on the other hand, engaged in a medical situation, are under duty to sustain life and keep a person alive, unless otherwise instructed by a living will, or a power of attorney. With express instruction to halt the effort to sustain life under defined circumstances, doctors may disconnect a respiratory machine. The heart stops. No life is taken. No charge ensues.

A person in a state of coma presents a complete absence of cognitive capacity. Extraordinary means can be deployed to sustain life, but there is no obligation to continue beyond the point of irreversible loss. When a brain ceases to function, there is no human being. The body can be disposed of.

What if grandma's state was such that her blood still flowed, her skin was still supple and pink, but she has no brainwave? She is a symbiosis of human and plant, strands of her plant and human lives persist. Bereft of a brainwave, however, she is done. Under the law, the cessation of cognitive function is the cessation of human life. Only congress, parliaments and assemblies of elected officials can alter this definition.

Martial law, laws during armed internal or international conflict

A range of legal issues emerges from the point of grandma's symbiosis as both plant and human; the point when grandma becomes a threat to public health.
In the threat of massive loss of human life, there is nothing to prevent the use of police powers and emergency powers to take the dual entity and place it somewhere safe.

Family and relatives of a deceased person may have wishes that authorities may try to honour. But ultimately, the State may override those wishes in the name of the common good. Moreover, absent any claims to a person or body, it is incumbent upon the State to dispose properly of a human body. By law, bodies unclaimed become public property and are consigned to a common grave.

The State's prerogative over such matters is all the more heightened as we debate the contagiousness of SEPS, (especially since news that the Bangkok doctors are now afflicted). What to do in this situation where the plant on the porch and the plant in grandma are the same and both present a harmful threat to society?

When foot-and-mouth disease broke out in England, containment demanded significant measures to quarantine, to vaccinate, and in many instances, to kill and cremate the animals.

In the case of SEPS, cremation stops the spread of the disease. The traditional rules will have to be modified. This may be painful for some cultures, which see cremation as akin to double murder, or at least as a social taboo.

This is a touchy issue in Liberia, a country of traditional Protestant Christians, who abhor the notion of cremation and would feel cheated out of a funeral if forced to cremate their dead. They see a second coming of their relatives reduced to ashes.

When people die, they may leave a living will that contains instructions on what should happen. Legislation defines how these instructions will be honoured by medical practitioners. Only through a living will could one manifest the intent to be planted, not cremated. A relative or person may defend their right to look after their deceased relative/surviving plant. If there is no societal harm, there is no problem in honouring such wishes. Today, when useful organs are harvested from a disposed body, heirs are entitled to the proceeds from the organs. Property rights belong to the heirs, who are simply abiding by the directions of the deceased.

According to one public health expert, many people in West Africa hold that the day one dies is the most important day of one's life. It must be done right, and it is obvious how people would be upset if it were not. West Africans have a tradition of observing a 42-day period after death, just as the Jews have Shiva.

Once disease is shown to be contagious, to any extent, it becomes a legal issue. When a person is still alive and carries the contagion, public health measures are required. Like Ebola in West Africa and SARS in Southern China, we are awaiting the next disease to cross the human divide and deliver another plague or Spanish influenza.

Whatever the vector of contagion is determined to be, the State will have every reasonable power to control it. Wherever something may be spreading, it must be shut down. The principle of *the greater good for the greater number* is the rule that applies.

All factories and workplaces could be closed to prevent disease from spreading, as was the case in Sierra Leone when a shutdown of three days was imposed, a difficult choice, and one that was hard for authorities to enforce. It prevented people from earning income and getting food. During those three days, special teams went from house to house to find hidden cases of Ebola. Ultimately, the general view was that forcing people to stay in their homes for three days was a useful containment measure.

However, in Liberia, there was a village near Monrovia, one of the poorest places on Earth, which registered a high degree of contagion. The government decided to build a perimeter preventing the population from leaving for an indefinite period. A riot ensued, and many escaped into the nearby areas, further spreading the disease.

How can such measures be balanced against the most fundamental of human rights such as the right to association, the right to free speech, the government's restriction of speech and laws of denunciation? In a war all sorts of measures can be taken to defeat an enemy, and the exercise of certain rights can be controlled in the interests of the greater good. The rules on the exercise of state power become very permissive, but they still must pass the test of reasonableness. When society is confronted with a deadly contagious disease, the rules can be analogized to those of armed conflict—known as 'international humanitarian law.' In peace the authorities cannot shoot someone unless he presents an imminent threat. In war, an enemy soldier can be shot while he sleeps because he is part of force that represents a continuing threat. In peace, you must have a warrant to enter a house. In war, you can blow up the house and kill the occupants if you have reason to believe that it is being used by an enemy for military purposes and you cannot reasonably eliminate the threat any other way. So it would be if SEPS were highly contagious and extreme measures were required to prevent its spread. However, there would have to be a balancing. The authorities would need to carefully discriminate between situations that presented a serious threat and those that did not. All reasonable precautions would need to be taken, and measures could not be taken that were disproportionate to the benefits to be gained. So the rules would be discrimination, precaution, and proportionality.

What was effective in fighting Ebola and the Plague? Would it be effective for SEPS to create a vegetation-free zone? In lieu of a garden, paving a lawn and painting it green may not be entirely aesthetically objectionable. Would the authorities need to compensate the home owner? Yes, if it was a permanent taking of the right to grow vegetation on one's property, but no if it was the temporary exercise of police powers to stop a contagion. As under martial law, there is no compensation to make up for the measures deemed necessary. The protection of immediate life is fundamental. If everyone turns into plants, there is no future. If 30% of the human population is attacked, the remaining 70% must be protected. Quarantined areas would be vegetation-free zones that would eventually lead to a drastic reduction in biodiversity.

But the Government can act, and it can act without asking us. *Who will bear the cost of all this?* There will be profound problems for the economy. Communities will be isolated; transportation, communication and all things essential to our trade and economy will break down. SEPS will wreak something far worse than the worst global depression.

How can remediation be paid for? There will be a breakdown of law and order, with a potential return to feudalism. There is a need to establish public order and protect people, and more than ever a need to control things. Where and how can we do this? In the past, the first reflex was to aim for the deepest pockets to sue, when the past afforded the luxury of knowing what we were going up against. Cigarette companies knowingly lied. It was all too obvious how and where to obtain an award of damages, even triple damages.

In US states, costs imposed on a community can be recovered by a state attorney general from the responsible party. The AG acts as *parens patriae* or as public parent for the affected community.

With SEPS, it is not so clear what we are dealing with, or who the culprit is. Consider the issue of chemical waste, and the dumping carried out by companies that actually met standards at the time. When later evidence showed the hazardous consequences on human health, those industries were taxed, as they were under the US 'super fund' program. The cost of remediation becomes a public taxation issue.

Would the plants' interests be taken into account in the balancing? Would they have standing like corporations that are persons under the law? One can legislate the protection of plants, just as we protect against cruelty to animals. Legislation can be enacted to confer on plants a status similar to that of a person. But in the absence of such legislation, they would not have legal standing.

The question becomes then: *are they people who are transformed into plants or people who were killed by plants?*

Under common law followed in the US, UK and some Commonwealth countries, one is not obligated to come to the assistance of a person in trouble, but if one begins to assist and the assistance fails, he or she can held liable. In these countries there are Good Samaritan laws to protect people who assist with good motives, even if they do more harm than good. This encourages assistance, but does not require it.

There is no requirement to protect or assist when brain function has stopped. Where there is a public health consequence, however, this may change.

If one were to become a contagious bamboo plant, but with a functioning brain, one would have to be kept away from others by quarantine.

Under human rights law, isolation may create a deprivation. Jeremy Bentham famously said that human rights are nonsense on stilts. In the 21st century they are more than that but only governments can define and enforce them.

Intentional killing is where the law and morality intersect. Here is a case where the greatest good for the greatest number is not the rule. But in war, one can intentionally kill fellow human beings. And capital punishment for the most serious crimes is not a violation of international law. What then of killing persons who carry contagions that will inevitably spread to the whole population unless they are immediately killed and their bodies destroyed? One is tempted to say that this would never be justified. But given the enormous risk to society as a whole, it could pass the test of proportionality. In any case, the value of human life would weigh very heavily in the analysis.

But what of lesser measures, such as denying plant-human hybrids the right to reproduce? The answer might be different depending on how fast the individual was producing seeds.

Once the discussion goes back to who is responsible for SEPS, where it came from, we could very well point to something that has no legal standing, and therefore there would be no one to sue. Where, then, are the points of infection? The points of infection have come from existing large expanses of vegetation on this planet.

Who facilitated the development of this enormous area of highly diverse systems of plants? The World Bank, Conservation International, the John Muir Society, to name a few. Society's tacit aiding and abetting via national parks is like supporting ISIS training camps.

Some people are infected, some people die, some reach a state of stable symbiosis. In such a context, there is a new class of hybrid people, part vegetable and part human. Of their own volition, with working minds, they may decide to advance their interests and claim they are a new species that ought to propagate and have rights because they are still human enough. In such a context, would this particular group that is not dead or completely incapacitated, not also constitute a public health menace?

We would need to quarantine them and protect ourselves. If they tried to break out, force could be justified.

Countries have differing views. In Mexico, the infected group may feel that it is in fact returning to its natural origins. Those infected are not doing any damage, and they are saving their own culture because they are returning to nature. What happens if we, in one particular country, consider that the deceased group will destroy humanity? Yet in countries such as Mexico, or Guatemala or Chile, some believe that SEPS is not a disease but something to be fully embraced.

Rules of isolation would apply, and quarantines must be respected. There is a legitimate concern of contagion. This is not like a Typhoid Mary or an Ebola carrier. If they are not contagious but simply strange, then the South Americans can still enjoy the freedom of movement. If they are somehow more contagious, quarantine is justified and the most minimally coercive measures must be taken to prevent their contagion from reaching others who are not.

It is fair to posit then that one group is being set aside. Their human rights are being curtailed because of something another group considers bad.

There will be two, if not more systems of science competing.

Based on our science, if they come to town and infect the town and are unable to turn into happy symbiotic creatures and are simply left to die, the state is justified to bar them from entering.

If they require something to help their condition, they should have the opportunity to get it.

This is similar to what happened when the HIV/AIDS epidemic began. To enter some countries in Europe, a blood test was required. Countries such as France required blood tests to determine if a person was HIV positive before issuing visas.

How many people had their temperature taken during the Ebola crisis? Airports implemented the use of thermal imagers and infrared cameras to detect high body temperatures and fevers.

What happens at the border is different from what can happen inside a state. People can be strip-searched at borders, but in their homes, they cannot be searched without a search warrant.

If one is infected by a plant or a plant is exploiting a human, it could have a long life cycle. It may not manifest itself for a long time, anywhere from 6 months to a year. One could carry the contagion and be crossing borders right, left and centre. As it stands, it may not be transmitted or contagious. The genetic material from the organism must be reproduced. Even if a person is forced to stay home and quarantined, flowers are produced, capsules are produced, and all of a sudden 10 000 seeds are produced. It can enter the stomach and not be rejected. Whatever it is, it is in the country and it is proliferating.

Intriguingly, in the case of Ebola, Nigeria was different from Liberia. Nigeria did an excellent job of isolating people, containing the virus, and monitoring them closely during the incubation period. So long as a specific period of time elapsed without any incidents, they were clear. SEPS is capable of going in all directions, hence the difficulty of conceiving a public health policy. Simply tracking it, as highlighted by the epidemiologist, is difficult.

Can one discriminate against plant/human hybrids? In the USA, the equal protection clause to the constitution is interpreted to make some forms of discrimination 'invidious' or almost never justified. The campaign for the Equal Rights Amendment, or ERA, was about entrenching sex or gender into an invidious classification. In order to justify such discrimination, a very heavy burden must be proven. Otherwise, one can discriminate between persons if such discrimination is reasonable: among students based on their test scores, among athletes based on their ability to run or jump.

The question is can we discriminate against someone who has only some of the attributes of a human? Under the law, given the impact, this is possible. They can be put in a separate place, and kept from disturbing others.

The more difficult issue emerges when the plant becomes a threat. Knowing what we know, and don't know, we would be heading into a war with many casualties.

6. *Civil Society and its Resources*

Professor Cronin observed that discussions thus far have elucidated two points of general agreement. SEPS can be understood as either plant-centric, or human-centric, both more or less exclusive of one another.

It has been clearly established that human laws emerged from humans, communities, nations, all of which are constructs. But in this epidemic the main actors, conscious or not, are plants. The outcome will be a sum of natural processes, rather than something to which we can impugn human-like motives, expectations and emotions.

Ultimately one could imagine a new equilibrium once plant life has achieved some dominance or symbiotic relationship with the human species. Even if that means that part of the human population is wiped out. If plants are responsible, and in the short term, they are the ones with far greater capacity to influence SEPS, there is little humans can respond to, other than discuss how far plants can go, what they are doing, and when they are doing it.

Still, from a human-based perspective, two things can be attempted. Firstly, determine whether or not the devastation wrought is such as to bring about a crisis of law and order, and render government incapable. If government succeeds in containing SEPS, it becomes a matter of public policy, one shaped by the kind of government in power, its legal instruments, its capacity to impose emergency legislation and measures for prevention.

The second scenario is that government is temporarily out of commission. On account of broken links, military and police forces are down (a corollary of broken communication or full blown pandemic). We would return to the imperative of identifying social groups that have resources located on the ground, within close enough proximity that they can mobilise. In such a context, we would proceed to an inventory of which groups have what.

Family and ethnic ties will become very important. Groups that are best positioned in such situations are people who can bond together easily, forge trust, and have pre-existing ties to be mobilized. They are not necessarily responsible for what happened; however, they have greater capacity to act than those who are dislocated, lack social connections and resources.

We privilege the smaller groups and ones that are connected with one another in various, informal ways. Sometimes, this refers as much to ethnic groups as it does to neighbourhoods. Neighbourhoods and regions are often very fragmented. Urban communities can be at each other's throats. We have a good sense that middle, upper-middle and upper class communities have protection; but that could break down, especially if electromagnetic communication fails.

Different fates will await different groups. Marx famously said that peasants have no capacity to act (being geographically dispersed). Those living in farming areas, or in isolation, may not have a set of resources to mobilize, nor would they necessarily need large amounts of resources to do so. Among smaller groups and communities, there will be differences in traits, particularly in levels of understanding. For those who face the greatest threat, the question is, how well organized can they be? To the extent that more localized groups become society's resource-bearers and mobilisers, the better their ability to process information, the better served the rest of the population will be.

This third scenario, an incapacitated government that will cede to smaller groups possessing differentiated characteristics and capacities to mobilise, resist and survive must be explored in detail. This discussion does not proceed to the exclusion of the first two scenarios: (1) that SEPS is entirely of the domain of plants and there is nothing humans can do, (2) government and rule of law remains sufficiently intact to act according to the principle of the greater good for the greatest number.

Under a third scenario, we must assess how groups will proceed intelligently and effectively. Take global warming and human reaction to it. In the beginning, no one knew where it came from, how it was caused, who to believe, or indeed if there was anything to believe. No one could initially fathom that climate change was attributable to human action. There was, and still is, a phase of denial. Those at the government level are particularly culpable of denial because they are not affected. To date, global warming has been most felt by island dwellers. Long-term, protracted denial therefore has been the easy and default option.

In the case of SEPS, given the prevalence of type 2 stomach flora, and the elevated risk of middle to upper-middle class people for high impact, the denial phase will be shortened because the decision makers are among the first infected.

The presumption of smaller family units acting rationally is predicated on strong connections between these groups to make a successful foray into solving the problem.

Where does that connective tissue come from?

Contemporary society (in the United States and elsewhere) has become individualistic and atomized, with little if no interaction among neighbours. This is a structural condition. For individuals and families to do anything, they would need another form of connection, such as being part of an ethnic group, to feel a sense of identity. Ethnic groups do not necessarily see that identity as the most enlightened marker when they act. But in the absence of any other group, ethnic groups will be one of the more obvious groups to emerge. Given the realities of American cities, neighbours tend to be of the same racial group and social class. Not all are necessarily Italian, Irish or Jewish, but they are segregated enough to share other markers that are more or less compatible. Ethnicity and other kinds of identity are built from various sources. Perhaps identity politics will make a vengeful comeback because this is all that will be left in the wake of SEPS.

Unless we see the emergence of a *Stand up for Non-Plant Infected Humanity!* movement. There would be a new group to demonise.

Yet if ethnic lines are the first drawn during the early stages of the SEPS crisis, they are not the only places where social solidarity is being built or can be built up. Research on social resilience in the wake of Hurricane Katrina revealed ways that people came together. General work on social resilience in the context of social disasters suggests that a key to success in surmounting disaster is whether one knows one's neighbours and talks to them. Ethnicity as an identifier of community and solidarity is dominant, but the connective tissues that bind a community can be defined much more broadly than that.

Interaction is much easier in the case of a disaster. An epidemic will be more terrifying than a natural disaster because lending assistance comes with exposure to the contagion. SEPS presents a much, much trickier situation.

The 'dominant group' will carry the expectation to do what government might do: reasonable things for those who are infected. The sick would be separated and treated. How can this be managed with informal associations? It will be hard. The tendency will be to ostracize and protect a group from contagion.

There is an abundance of literature on how social movements can be formed rapidly through social media. In the case of

SEPS, it is difficult if not impossible because social media is seen as conducive to spreading the disease. There is an implication that connections will be tougher to maintain. TV will likely be shut down for public health reasons.

One hypothesis is that smaller, rural, farm communities, where everyone knows everyone else will emerge as well organized, tightly knit communities. Bonds and trust are pre-existing; remoteness of locale tends to afford autonomy of action. Such groups are most likely to have a good response.

Countering this view, however, is a recurrence of what happened during mobilization around AIDS. When middle class white gay men were infected, they successfully mobilized their resources because a segment of the group worked within the State machinery. They had privileged access to the Centers for Disease Control and Prevention (CDC), Centers for Medicare and Medicaid Services (CMS) and the Food and Drug Administration (FDA). It mattered not whether the outbreak was caused by sex workers, drug addicts, blacks or Latinos, a vitriolic debate eventually reduced to silence when the disease was traced back to a little Caucasian boy following a transfusion. The decisive factor was that the group infected wielded capacity. They were successful in opening the channels to change policy.

After mobilization, other struggling groups were able to benefit from the efforts, but certainly not at the same level. Within that gay community, there were groups that had more resources than others. They fought for them. When white middle-class gay men in New York, San Francisco and Chicago were mobilizing, they were thinking only of themselves. Among black men, AIDS was viewed as something that happens to white men, not them. Once the disease hit their group, they lacked the resources to mobilize, and it became evident they were confronted with an additional layer of challenge, how to prioritise their problems. Already disadvantaged by other ills, this group had to choose not only what and how to mobilize, but around which issue: schooling, poverty, jobs.

What this proves is that the people with resources are the ones who will go furthest and will survive. The marginalized, the ones with fewer resources, are always, in evolutionary parlance, the weakest link.

If small community groups are to operate on their own and develop associations across the neighbourhood, will they really be able to succeed? Conventional thinking suggests they would be less effective because they have relied more on elite contacts across greater distances. They may not have the same kind of ties within their own community to mobilize people and provide care.

A case in point is opium addiction. Once it became apparent that white middle class people were dying from opioid overdose, it was suddenly seen as a scourge and resources were committed to eradicating it. It was a problem otherwise previously linked with criminality. Opium addicts drew scorn and moral judgment. The problem was reframed when the problem became white.

Who has ties and resources when other ties and resources fall apart? Criminals and criminal gangs. The people best positioned are people who are brought together and kept together for illicit purposes. The Resource Mobilization theory stresses communication and prior links, entirely consistent with the ties that bond criminal groups, even if they happen to take on the form of threat, loyalty and fear. When the Soviet Union collapsed, the sector of society best equipped to embrace free enterprise was the mafia. A breakdown of public order would lead to these pathological developments.

Some model will have to work. The more small and close knit a community, the greater the chance that volunteerism will prevail. There will likely be a sort of coalition between community and criminal gangs, the former (with luck) injecting some amount of discipline into the latter.

A haunting example from the West African Ebola epidemic brings into sharp focus the level of societal antipathy that will manifest. Liberia was under-equipped to deal with swift spread of the disease. Yet when workers in white protective suits came to take away the bodies of loved ones, villagers in Liberia were appalled. Public campaigns to educate the population on safety measures, care centres and health protocol fell abysmally flat. Liberians were so profoundly estranged from their government that any public health warning was instantly construed as a ploy to dupe and deceive. What became understood, if never stated out loud, was that government corruption was terrible. This fact was confirmed quietly in the corridors of international organisations, and later on quite loudly by investigative news outlets. Liberians did not trust government messages because they could not believe a word the government said. Whatever the government said was instantly put down to ulterior motives.

It is suggested that there is a link between this and the massive protest votes for Brexit, an example of entrenched government distrust. People were voting no to other groups of people. After the banking crisis, in which so many ordinary people lost their homes and savings, no one was put in jail, no one was held responsible. These are signs of a system breakdown.

Borders may disintegrate. Rural communities, Type 2 gut flora people (see item 2, Epidemiological Overview), and farmers, will be concentrated in areas such as the Greater Mekong, and the rest of the population will live separately. SEPS will have generated a fundamental socio-political change, and all of the world centres of power will be shifted.

Those in farming will not be just subsistence farmers, but people engaged in a variety of activities, something that will change when power shifts. Subsistence farmers will have and use connections to strengthen social ties, in ways unseen in the cities. The middlemen who are fluent enough to play the game of the metropolis and barter with the locals for rice, rattan, and all manner of resources will be indispensible. There will be a selective impact on political centres of power.

Multinationals will no longer be able to operate in the absence of government entities, borders, and segregated groups. There will be no way to work remotely, as digital media and computers exacerbate the disease. People would still use computers and weigh the risk of being completely cut off from communication, rather in the way that the Petrushka group decided to contact an epidemiologist. People will take to protective jumpsuits, or return to the use of typewriters and landline telephones.

What will occur during a SEPS crisis in a world with no borders? Thinking locally and knowing that the Massachusetts State government is sufficiently corrupt, people will start fleeing the cities. Where would they go? Would properties be taken over? In this part of the world one would head for Vermont, even if it is replete with forests. More people in Vermont are accustomed to subsistence and small agriculture. There is less corporate and less monoculture farming. Vermont holds particular attraction, given its cold winters, slow-growing vegetation, and inhospitable climate to fast-growing bamboo. There are fewer electromagnetic fields.

During other outbreaks such as Ebola and AIDS, there were attempts to control borders. In 2010, a document called the International Health Regulations (IHR) was released which provides countries with guidelines on detecting and responding to health threats during international travel, whether to keep a person on a plane, or unload them and take them to a hospital. There are rules and provisions, but they require countries to have capacities, which many do not have. The rules were agreed upon by all countries. Yet when the West African crisis occurred, travel was restricted much more severely than necessary.

As people start to flee, some will be let in, others kept out, particularly those with the wrong intestinal flora. If government is sufficiently intact, and if there is enough expertise, scientists and academics will figure things out. It is hoped that more developed institutions of civil society will remain, such as teachers unions and the like, which will become poles of attraction. If the matter of who to let in and who to keep out is handled correctly, the rebuilding of society will start from the periphery. It will happen in places that are developed enough to become centres of expertise and serious policymaking, free of infection, or infected to a lesser degree.

Civil society will have to promote an activist response that focuses on SEPS itself. Regarding family structure, conventional teaching on sex and reproduction will not be enough. If a person is presenting symptoms, will they continue or stop having intercourse? What if a woman is pregnant? How does infection affect fertility? There will be a Zika-style effect on pregnancy; women will think twice about their reproduction.

Since the invited speaker had not survived, the chair introduced this item. Two contrasting groups of humans (subsistence farmers and the very wealthy) were likely to prevail. Under such circumstances a few art forms would probably survive. During the 14th century outbreak of the Plague, a group fled to the hills above Florence, where they gathered and told each other stories, as recounted by Boccaccio in the Decameron. At the other end of society are the Scottish ballads and folktales, concise accounts of noble treachery and supernatural events. They were passed on for centuries by word of mouth. In a major collapse there will be no more opera or cinema. Indeed, even items such as the Decameron might be in difficulty, depending as they do on someone to print, type or copy them out. Societal meltdown would leave only oral tradition.

On religion, the chair could speak, diffidently, of only two forces: Christianity, from the inside, and Buddhism from outside. Curiously, the index case of SEPS is in south central Siberia, perhaps the only place where historic communities of both Christians and Buddhists live: Orthodox Old Believers who had fled the persecution of Ivan the Terrible, and Buddhists who first appeared there when T'ang monks journeyed west.

The major religions will almost certainly survive, even the strictest of them showing flexibility and ingenuity when it needs to encompass new circumstances and draw new congregations: witness the circle on the Celtic cross, a symbol of Irish sun-worship incorporated in the central sign of the Christianity, and the Burmese inclusion of the Nats, local deities, in the national Buddhist pantheon.

Believers, especially among migrant populations – and SEPS is causing vast, complex migrations – will tend to trust their religious leaders more than the civil authorities. Migrant groups from Asia and Africa to Europe call to mind the suspicions harboured by Irish Catholics who fled the potato famine in the 19th century and stuck close to the Church, an essential part of their lives and identities. They were not famous for their civic sense and found the social setup in their new homes completely foreign. It took a couple of generations, at least, for them to integrate. The same can be expected of new migrants. The stronger the religious affiliation, the longer it will take to integrate. But to integrate with what? And what is the nature of religious affiliation?

Second question first. There would seem to be several dimensions to it. At base there is the Golden Rule, the Western version of which is 'Do as you would be done by', which does warrant interference in the lives of others, who might not agree with your notion of the good. The Buddhist version is something like 'Do not do to others what you would not wish done to yourself', and here the problem – if it is one – is a certain passivity.

Next is the style of devotion, though not style of a superficial kind. Both Christianity and Buddhism run the gamut from austere and cerebral to florid and emotional. In Buddhism this goes from Zen at one end to the riotous Hindu imagery of Tantric Buddhism at the other. In Christianity, Cistercian abbeys are the epitome of austerity, closer to Lutheranism than to Sicilian or Andalusian Baroque, which in their way seem more akin to the excesses of Tantra.

The third dimension is the relation to civil authorities, which is governed by response to specific issues affecting the status of the religion and the integrity of its people. In this respect one Christian sect, and even one priestly order within that sect, can run the political gamut; western Jesuits, famous or infamous for seeking influence at the top of society, were on both sides in the Cold War.

The underside of this third dimension is corruption. The Catholic Church has proven almost hopelessly corrupt, as witness the paedophile scandal (and see Matthew 18:6).

So what can we expect? Buddhists and Christians will be found at every point on that three-dimensional space. For Buddhists, we expect a certain acceptance that the crisis is part of the natural order. Groups that are being infected first will view the occurrence as karmic retribution. Some Christians too will see an element of divine retribution, and also some breakdown in the mandate of Genesis to maintain dominion over the earth and all living creatures. Any group that is sheltered from a sudden outbreak will be tempted to see itself as morally vindicated – though such a response is not restricted to those of a religious disposition.

In such times of crisis, many turn to religion. During the 14th century outbreak of the Plague, the role of religious institutions was crucial. There was fanaticism, self-flagellation and persecution of other creeds. At the same time, in the absence of any formal system of governance or public health institutions, the Church was *the* institution that provided care, hospitals, places of refuge, last rites, all manner of social integrative functions. During the AIDS epidemic in Mexico, the Catholic Church was conspicuously silent. But there were known cases of a few Jesuits (again the Jesuits) who resided on the border in order to take in transgender people and open the door to health and medical services.

To return to the initial question: what should these religions integrate with? The only certain answer, when central government is in doubt, is civil society, an answer which returns us to the discussion of item 6. Like neighbourhood and ethnicity, religion adds a stratum of social allegiance. In this respect different religions, and different national variants thereof, will have their own contributions to make. North American

Catholics are strong on adoption and opposed to abortion, though they tend to neglect the elderly; Latino and Mediterranean Catholics retain strong family bonds and shore them up, as is now necessary, by drafting in home help from poorer countries. Jewish communities have strong traditions of mutual support. It is women who do most of this work, and the old people who suffer neglect are, for the most part, women also. Religion is not free of misogyny.

We need to know more about what the other great spiritual traditions might offer – the various forms of animism in particular.

In China, there are sacred places, mountains and forests. Such places are described in the story, *The King of Trees* by Ah Cheng. During the Cultural Revolution a group of students is sent to the countryside for re-education, instructed to clear the mountain of 'useless trees' and fill the primeval land with 'useful trees.' Atop the mountain stands one huge tree. An old man in the village warns against cutting it down, lest something terrible occur, at which the leader of the students berates him for spreading superstition. The trees are cleared progressively, supplanted by commercial saplings, until it comes time to axe the last and largest one standing. The old man stands with it, defending it. Eventually, the party secretary orders him to cede to the young revolutionaries. They are the future of the country and know what they are doing. The man moves. It takes several days to cut down the ancient tree. The man becomes weaker and weaker, until he dies. The students bury the man where the tree once stood. Later, the students return to find the coffin being pushed out of the soil. New trees are growing around the burial site. They decide to cremate the body. At this point, everyone in the village is distressed. All the villagers, except for the students, knew of the man and his relationship to the tree. They spread the man's ashes over where the tree once stood. Quickly after, the soil is covered with flowers. Tinged with Taoist-Confucian ideas, the story contrasts traditional culture and beliefs in the village with sweeping revolutionary progressive ideas.

It is assumed that movements within and among major religions will work to help the afflicted and provide some kind of social cohesion. It is further assumed that certain religious people – some Buddhists and more animists – will go so far as to welcome the transformations caused by SEPS. However, it is clear that SEPS causes revulsion – overpowering nausea is a frequent sign in sufferers, and those who are not infected tend to fear those who are.

We must therefore ask what role will be played by art in its surviving forms. In one respect art is no different from religion: its practitioners will support or fight the powers that be, or they will follow an inner voice that has nothing to say about the current catastrophe.

Part 5 of this report reviews the response of society under the rule of law; part 6 considers how residual human society might operate even if central and local government breaks down. This 7th part must contemplate what happens if humanity loses its ancient definition. This is where the arts come into their own.

The SEPS epidemic is just starting. In the initial phases, it is advancing clumsily, brutally, killing the host. But it may evolve to a point where it does not, such that the human genome as well as the plant genome is maintained. A dualism will emerge in a blending of plant and human genetic material. The offspring will be human, in a very tight relationship with plant life.

Amidst all the fear, art should help envisage different, various streams of life. The arts will give strength to the notion of 'difference'. Artists will delve into the minds of past writers, such as J.G. Ballard, who posited different species and structural collapse. They will look to the many poems that express a degree of acceptance of humankind's metamorphosis and synergy with plant life. In communities, people will rally around what they believe defines them, something that forges an identity – a function art shares with religion. But positive representation of the new being in formation is for the arts alone. It can be high art or something as simple as everyday utensils.

8. *Sustaining Communities*

Professor Laura Frader asked what can be learned about managing SEPS from the resource mobilization that occurs, or that does not occur, particularly within communities which lack resources during natural disasters.

Questions about community, polity, communications and education in a post-SEPS society should be taken not as a problem of preservation, but as a matter of resilience and civic sustainability. This is not about being reactive. The response will lie in the building of connective tissue within society in a manner that is protective.

One of the issues that emerges is whether this epidemic invites a conceptual revolution about the nature of community, the nature of social relations and whether they need to be transformed. Given the extent of SEPS, it is unlikely that we can go on as before, and we need to think about ways of sustaining ourselves.

As a starting point, it is worth recalling three historic epidemics and disasters. The bubonic plague of 1346–1353 is estimated to have killed between 75 and 200 million people, between 30% and 60% of Europe's population. Jews, foreigners, Roma and lepers were all blamed for the Plague and persecuted. In the absence of government apparatus and public health institutions, religious institutions and beliefs played a tremendous role in care. People who survived benefited. Workers wages rose. Feudal institutions crumbled with the demand for wage labour. Subsequent outbreaks, from then till now, have prompted the creation of public health institutions.

The Spanish flu pandemic of 1918 is estimated to have killed between 30 and 40 million people in a single year. It has been described as the worst epidemic in history, affecting perhaps one fifth of the world's population. Over a quarter of all Americans were infected and nearly 675 000 of them died. One estimate puts flu mortality at ten times that of combat deaths in World War One. It was most deadly for people between the ages of 20 and 40 (we do not yet know which age groups are most vulnerable to SEPS). The speed of onset was extraordinary. From first sign to death could take less than a day. The mechanism is what we now call a cytokine storm: an intense surge of white cell production that releases certain chemical, which attack the organs, with fatal outcome. It is what happens during sepsis, or when people fall prey to severe nosocomial infections. The body kills itself.

The reach of Spanish flu was global. Even in areas where mortality was low, so many people were incapacitated that much of daily life was hampered. In some communities, people shut down commercial activity or customers were instructed to leave their orders outside, in vain attempts to contain the disease. There were reports that healthcare workers could not tend to the sick; gravediggers were too sick to bury the dead. Mass graves were dug by steam shovel and bodies were buried without coffins. With the shutdown of industry and commerce, the labour force was severely reduced. The impact on the global economy was massive.

The flu epidemic, as far as most historians are concerned, did not cause government breakdown. Since governments were already on a war footing they were able to mobilize resources, and people readily complied with government instructions on quarantine and other public health measures. It was a defining moment in the emergence of public health, certainly in the USA.

In all this the healthcare industry progressed well in terms of its own development and prominence, to the extent that it succeeded in dealing with the disease. Women benefited from this shift, in that greater access to higher education in this period allowed them to occupy caring and nursing roles.

The third historical case is not an epidemic but a natural disaster: Hurricane Katrina of 2005. Many of those affected were poor and people of colour, living near or in the worst affected areas. Buildings were destroyed. There was social breakdown, some looting of essential goods, and a certain hysteria that was amplified by the media.

Sometimes such disasters afford opportunities to pull people together, but the connective tissue that binds is the ultimate determinant; the tsunami of 2004 is credited with ending the Indonesian offensive in Aceh, which had cost a quarter of a million lives; but it did not stop the war in Sri Lanka.

After Hurricane Katrina, many government and quasi-government responses were inadequate, despite the existence of evacuation plans. Eventually the National Guard was mobilized to come in and keep the peace. At the same time, and this is an important lesson that can be transferred to the case of SEPs, an extraordinary amount of community resilience came to the fore. People were rescuing and helping each other. In the face of an inadequate government response, Katrina proved a model of community solidarity, exemplified especially by African American communities and black churches.

It is clear the notion of resilience must be part of the response. The previous discussion centred on social cohesion *within* social groups. This discussion of past disasters, natural and epidemic, forces us to consider the power of social cohesion *across* social groups. There is potential for a positive response, a kind of creative energy that is channelled when dealing with a disaster or an epidemic. All of this requires rethinking what community is, something that necessarily must cut across racial and ethnic groups.

We do not know how badly SEPS has disrupted levels and systems of governance. If public officials are affected by SEPS, as they must be, a degree of government breakdown is guaranteed. Government offices will be shut, social services have disappeared or are vastly reduced. Law and order have diminished capacity. Epidemics and natural disasters cause disruption and can give rise to violence.

The rules of armed conflict may apply in respect of this epidemic. Government is empowered to take measures without popular approval. There is nothing to prevent the police from coming in, burying bodies, burning plants and imposing quarantines. This is one way in which the State, or what remains of it, exercises control. In the case of SEPS, we need to know how much government breakdown has occurred. If a complete breakdown is averted, with some structure of civil government or organized society still operational, and the remaining 50% population still healthy, there will be a response. What kind of response? It has to include research, data gathering, quarantine, and mobilized medical services. It will begin locally.

Levels of collapse will vary from country to country. Is there any sense of some countries or places doing a good or better job already? It should be easier for a small and wealthy country to deal with a disaster than it is for a large and poor country, although not always: Japan did not deal with Fukushima particularly well. In Detroit, the eventual response to industrial blight was sustainable urban farming. There must be places where these things are handled well, but they are not garnering headlines. Societies will rebuild from the periphery. The notions of centre/periphery of social systems will be transformed.

In terms of communications, given evidence that electromagnetic fields exacerbate the spread of SEPS, people are thinking twice before using cell phones, computers and digital equipment. New systems of communication in the age of SEPS will have to be devised, perhaps something akin to how plants and the root systems of trees communicate to help each other survive, forming a symbiotic relationship with fungi in the ground. The fungus explores the soil, sends mycelium through the soil, picks up nutrients and water, returning it to the plant, and exchanges those nutrients for photosynthate. The roots are, in effect, fixing carbon, trading it for substances needed for growth. The forest has an underground mycorrhizal network that connects the root systems of trees, allowing them to pass on data, nutrients, and warnings of encroaching pests and disease. It has been noted that plants can communicate also by releasing pheromones into the atmosphere, warning neighbours to secrete more tannin, for example, in order to repel attack from bark beetles. Could immunity to SEPS be activated by ascertaining which pheromones can turn a system of protection on or off?

In terms of social rather than biological communication, we can take it to extremes. A Swedish government policy of the 1970s sought to make everyone self-sufficient. As a result, people died alone in tiny studios, unburied because next-of-kin were unreachable and the bills of suicide victims had been set up for automatic payment. In contrast, a community in Okinawa, Japan, started a healthcare programme after the Second World War, designating one healthcare advocate for every five people, to check neighbours constantly. It is still running. Medical healthcare is put on equal footing with social wellbeing. This community has registered the highest average age in the world.

SEPS does throw people back on their own resources, but rather than total autonomy, we should prefer something like the one-to-five ratio of healthcare worker to public. Those who are immune to SEPS would be the key players, keeping contact through home visits and minimal electronic communication. Of course, the hysteria and fake news that follows this type of crisis will have to abate before a module-to-module structure can be set up.

Education

There are two things to focus on: the rebuilding of institutions and the content of education. Educational institutions can foster civic sustainability, providing cultural capital and cultural competency. They can help to deal with the ostracism of people who are infected, and to understand the dimensions of the disease and what to do about it. Schools play a crucial role as sustainers of community and places of refuge. Civic sustainability can be taught. Schools must foster social integration, though with SEPS we do not know how many people are able and available.

Education will cover practical things. Schools should teach students how to grow food, get water, farm locally, and use methods that are biologically based and aligned with the Natural Step principles.

Yet is should not be forgotten that after Hurricane Katrina, the public school system in New Orleans ceased to exist. Charter schools took over. Given that public education in the US is broken, SEPS could well destroy it. Schools that rely on local property taxes will become even more fragile. School funding would be decided through the courts, if they still work.

In 1953, a catastrophic storm in The Netherlands led to a trillion-dollar public works program that remains in place today. Without that storm, they would not have the system of locks, dams, walls and gates that are effectively defending the country. In the US, there are only floodwalls. As global sea levels rise, we will have to adapt. Systems have been conceived for the survival of society, and we must identify where and what they are.

It is important to view civic sustainability and resilience as pre-emptive, protective measures that form the basis of a long-term response. Reactive measures, as we now see, are not sufficient.

Assuming that there is recovery, changes will occur somehow in the long term. There will be nodes of creative adaptation and long-term thinking. SEPS has led to assumptions about things breaking down, people reacting in unwise and unproductive ways. We are now challenged to think about ourselves in nature, and the shift in thinking should focus on achieving good outcomes from bad situations. There will be some selection. There are places that react badly, along with places that contained prior conditions conducive to better adaptation. Those places must be identified so that they become models that spread and replicate.

Civic education will be a long-term measure, just like public health measures after the Spanish flu epidemic. There will be a return to the foundational requirements of living in civil society. This must include social commitment to a progressive taxation system in replacement of the current global evasion mechanisms for the wealthy. The social backlash against the current system has been manifest in Brexit and in the USA.

There will be a massive disturbance to this system and the most basic skills in acquiring values will be re-taught through civic education. It has been suggested that SEPS will spur a return to the bartering system.

People have to learn how to critically read newspapers and watch TV (assuming it survives). There are courses aimed at sharpening critical thinking on where and how to look for things. There will have to be renewed investment in civic education to teach people how to identify and value the truth, and how to identify a hoax.

In the case of Hurricane Katrina, everyone knew that New Orleans was below sea level, yet no one seems to have thought, *what are we going to do if...?* SEPS was not predicted; but its connection to the environment is understood, which puts it technically on the radar. Pre-emptive measures come into play.

From what we know, there is a type of intestinal flora that confers immunity. The flora composition changes rapidly as bacteria pass through the gut. Genes can be exchanged. We should be studying what environment people are living in and especially what they are eating. It is clear that characterizing the gut flora of a human is tedious and expensive. Therefore, what humans are eating must be characterized and understood. The added challenge of course, is that we also do not know what we are eating. There are so many different types of intestinal flora; the majority will predominate according to what substrate they have to live off.

There is now an opportunity to move to a food system that is not based on chemicals. A more local food system will have to make up for the massive breakdown of supply chains. Humans depend on food coming from across the world. We must learn to rally around those who know how to do local farming. Equilibrium with SEPS will be achieved through our food intake.

It has been said that if only three systems could be changed—the food system, the energy system and the financial system—many problems would be solved. Now is our chance.

9. *Conclusion: Ecosystems*

Dr Hammond said that what we are eating is fewer and fewer different crops, tainted with more and more different chemicals. In our pursuit of agro-industrial efficiency and effectiveness we have destroyed half the planet's topsoil in the last 150 years, taking carbon out of the ground and lodging it in the air and oceans. Photosynthesis sustains all life, but 40% of its primary production is now monopolized by humans.

US farmers use the herbicide glyphosate, which inhibits plant growth, and atrazine, which does the opposite, provoking plant hormones to grow the plants to death. These products spread with the hydrological cycle as far as the Arctic, where their concentration in the breast tissue of women is the highest on earth. Remember Rachel Carson's observation in *Silent Spring*, that birds were not hatching because hormonal changes had made the eggshells fragile. The US Environmental Protection Agency (EPA) has now found atrazine in 90% of all drinking water tested. Seventy-five per cent of all surface water has atrazine in it. Levels far lower than current permitted limits disrupt the human hormonal system. A direct link to cancer is suspected.

Atmospheric carbon now stands at 400 parts per million; 300 million years ago it was as high, though at that time there were no ice caps, so no danger of a catastrophic rise in sea levels that would take out, among other things, yet more topsoil.

'The soil is the great connector of lives, the source and destination of all. It is the healer and restorer and resurrector, by which disease passes into health, age into youth, death into life. Without proper care for it we can have no community, because without proper care for it we can have no life.' [5]

---

[5] Wendell Berry, *The Unsettling of America: Culture and Agriculture* (1977).

The deterioration of the soil and stultification of our diet have damaged and impoverished our microbiome, leaving us much more open to challenge by species low down the food chain. It has been suggested that SEPS is a rebellion staged by plants. Perhaps, in terms of the ecosphere, it would be helpful to view it as something that is succeeding because it begins to redress the carbon balance; a return of the pendulum. Nature wants her carbon back in the form of vegetable and microbial diversity.

Efficiency and effectiveness have their place in Nature's economy, but diversity and redundancy, which make for resilience, seem to be at least as important.

A system with several ways of doing the same thing and many copies of the same item is unlikely to be destroyed by a single fire, flood or earthquake. The plant community is able to recover after devastation and can reflexively resort to ways of re-sprouting, re-nourishing and re-growing protective bark. Wetlands are able to respond after flooding. There are also responses to extraordinary events such as those caused by global warming. But natural ecosystems can respond only up to a certain level. At times systems are pushed over a threshold, such as a change in the whole water regime, or drought.

Sustainability and alignment between human and natural complex systems, especially as these systems adapt to change, are the cornerstones of the resilience paradigm.

In agriculture, resilience depends on the carbon in the soil. Part of what provides that carbon is diverse agriculture and an ecosystem with a multitude of plant species. When there is a high level of diversity among plant species, plants undergo and adapt to change on different cycles and at different levels. All of these species serve as diverse soil microbiome communities.

In urban societies, people are spending 90% of their time indoors. We have effectively disconnected from nature. To keep us connected and healthy, both mentally and physically, humans need to think about the need for nature and integrate this need into our way of life.

Biophilia is a concept that was introduced by Erich Fromm, in the book *The Art of Loving*. It was expounded in the book *Biophilia* by biologist Edward O. Wilson. It is about designing places and the way we live to ensure a tangible connection with Nature. We are drawn to Nature in art and architecture, and we are physically healthier and have stronger immune systems when our lives are more connected to Nature. In hospitals, people heal faster when they have a view of nature and are connected to it. Businesses are realizing that people are staying longer at work; there is slower turnover and less absenteeism when the environment is connected to nature. Immediate reduction in stress hormones has been detected in people living in an urban area when they walk past a green vacant lot. There is an increase in attentiveness. Certain nature areas foster creativity. The Japanese have a tradition called *Forest Baby*. To improve an immune system and increase killer t-cells, babies are nurtured in forests where they experience physical improvement in wellbeing.

Humans are in nature. Nature is needed for our physical and mental health. With SEPS we would face disaster should we opt to see plants as enemies.

There must be a focus on how to create solutions that align with sustainable practices, and that align with creating more resilient systems from within and without. These principles of built-in resilience, the need of nature for survival and wellbeing must be incorporated into solutions for societies, governance, and education.

As a final note, key principles of sustainable ways to create systems have been identified. There is school of thought, *The Natural Step*, started by the Swedish doctor Karl-Henrik Robert, who became alarmed at increased rates of childhood cancer. He brought together scientists from all fields, and they identified the following core principles:

(1) Do not remove substances from the earth's crust and release them into the atmosphere at rates faster than they can be absorbed. We can still use oils and metals, but not at a rate faster than the natural recycle rate.

(2) Do not put things into the atmosphere that nature cannot recycle or break down. There are now 80 000 man-made chemicals that have been released into the environment and which have never been tested for effects on human health. Nature cannot recycle them because they are not recognized as anything that Nature ever created.

(3) Do not destroy or manipulate natural ecosystems that provide us services required for the regeneration of healthy soil, water and forests.

(4) Ensure social equity. We cannot achieve any level of sustainability if it is not accessible and fair to all.

Observance of these principles would probably have prevented SEPS; they can surely mitigate its effects.

(Transcript)

20250131 <u>Note for the Record</u>

<u>Procedural</u>

Tedious title, wrong file number or date, handwritten — in English unfortunately; a draft in an exotic language would certainly have lain untranslated for a number of years even though it has been carefully placed in the public access division of the Assembly archive. Content of this first paragraph, which is always scanned by the electronic archivist for such metadata as can be found, will follow the method used by one person in Czechoslovakia (metadata there: refers to a defunct State) who got news past the censors to a friend abroad by starting his letter with a paragraph from an official report on paper quality (another term to tag) and underlining the occasional dull and irrelevant term throughout the text. On the assumption that the same technique works here, to business.

The Cape Cod report did get to the Assembly, which duly suppressed it. A summary was read to delegates and the document was destroyed for safety reasons. It was decided to proceed with Plan A, which will fail. Here's why and what to do about it next time.

Institutions: despotism, aristocracy, communism, democracy. I'm only a clerk of court filing a last NFTR before I decamp, so don't expect subtlety or footnotes. Some institutions were meant to be weak, others obsolesce or complicate in time. Some just seem to happen. Despotism is the strongest because strength is its sole purpose. Communism

collapsed with the Soviet Union. Don't tell
me it wasn't a genuinely communist state,
it's what there was and it didn't work. And
don't talk to me about communist China, that's
the Rotary Club with guns. Democracy would
appear to have taken a bow. There's the US
Constitution, Swiss banks, and Norway — heaven
help us — to tell us if we're corrupt. In
liberal democracy only three things are needed:
the rule of law, freedom of the press, and
democratic institutions. Needed for what? For
business. And what if you're not in business?
And if you are — do you really need them? If
you're not in business reality is TV and duty
is a game. You watch sport, right? You know all
about it and maybe you even used to hit a ball.
But now you let other people do that for you.
Same with politics, and if you don't like their
faces or their talk, you flip channels. Till
one day one of two things happens: you change
channels as usual but it's the same face you
see each time; or the other channels annoy you
so much that you stick to the feed you like.
Stuff happens. One day it happens to you and you
wonder why. In the long run, the institution
you want is aristocracy, entitlement inherited
from some species of pirate, kept in the
clan with the myth of better blood or better
brains, superior tact or education. But don't
get too clever, or make sure you've got clever
camouflage, preferably of the democratic sort.
It's a mild milieu for those and such as those.

But as of today it isn't mild on plants. No
international travel without a visa, no visa
without a chlorophyll detector on your mobile.
If detected, quarantine with or without your
entourage, surgery where available for those
who can afford it, cremation when the brain

does not respond to stimulus. Prophylactic
deforestation. Cross-border agricultural trade
in genetirylla modified organisms only.

My colleagues say I've got more physical, and
it's true. More hugs and handshakes, and I
stand closer to them when I speak, as if I'd
suddenly become a southerner. And whereas I'd
always been shy of the great and good I've
been using my position, in the Assembly hall,
to importune heads of mission, ambassadors
and Heads of State. 'Did you drop this paper?
Not yours? Oh, I'm sorry.' 'Excuse me, didn't
we meet in Singapore?' 'Excellency, could you
introduce me to that goodwill ambassador?
Haven't I seen her on TV? I need an autograph.'
Autotroph more like. I've been having dreams.
No other signs, but they're so persistent it
can't mean anything else. There's no sound, but
it isn't silence. I can't see but I feel light,
not just its warmth. When I say I feel I mean
touch taste and smell but merged and — here's
the thing — disaggregated. It's not that I have
no control but rather there isn't a controlling
I. There's input from above and about, solar
of course, but a lot of crosstalk with other
autotrophs. Below it's fungal. Does that mean
it's fungible? Among roots that are felt as
connected, and with some that clearly are not.
At times there's more going on among neighbours
than between root and branch. When the
eucalyptus is in season there's an overjoying
sense of sexual longing and fulfillment. Nothing
individual about it, nothing invidious. The
notion of species makes no sense, even the
other kingdoms get caught up in it, bugs and
little birds. But not the humans. Except in
dreams, and even there, there's a calculus that
will assess but will not share. Is it one or

the other? I mean is the iron/magnesium divide
unbridgeable (there's something in the Cape
Cod report about haemoglobin and chlorophyll).
This would mean that the brain would have to
die before the autotroph could function. Or
is symbiosis possible? If (a), then as Chuck
Peters put it, 'plants bat last' and we're
gone. If (b) who knows? Siberia here I come.